HUNT CLUB MANAGEMENT GUIDE

Skyhorse Publishing books may be purchased in bulk
at special discounts for sales promotion, corporate
gifts, fund-raising, or educational purposes. Special
editions can also be created to specifications. For
details, contact the Special Sales Department,
Skyhorse Publishing, 307 West 36th Street, 11th
Floor, New York, NY 10018 or
info@skyhorsepublishing.com.

Skyhorse® and Skyhorse Publishing® are registered
trademarks of Skyhorse Publishing, Inc.®, a Delaware
corporation.

Visit our website at www.skyhorsepublishing.com.

10 9 8 7 6 5 4 3 2 1

Library of Congress Cataloging-in-Publication Data
is available on file.

ISBN: 978-1-62873-690-8

Printed in China

HUNT CLUB MANAGEMENT GUIDE

Building, Organizing, and Maintaining Your Clubhouse or Lodge

by J. Wayne Fears

Skyhorse Publishing

Contents

It is like owning a place
in the country but
at a fraction of the cost.

INTRODUCTION

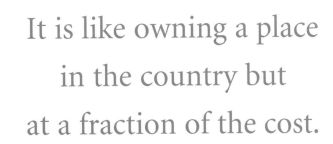

I t started in Texas and spread across the South. Then it spread up the Rocky Mountain states. Now they are springing up throughout the United States No, it is not a new chain of taco stands; it's the practice of leasing private land by a group for hunting.

Hunters in the United States of today face problems that their forefathers could not have conceived. In their day, hunting lands were easily found, most game species were abundant, and landowners were willing to grant hunting permission to almost any asking hunter. Now, the population explosion has changed all this. Our cities are growing, and the fields and forests that used to be open for hunting are becoming less available. Because of land shortage, hunters are grouping together, forming hunting clubs, to lease hunting rights on private land. If properly done, a membership in a hunting club can be one of a hunter's most prized possessions. Improperly done, it can become a nightmare.

I became involved in leasing hunting land back in the 1970s and early 80s, when I managed the Forest Recreation Division of Gulf States Paper Corp., a forest products company in Alabama. The company owns 500,000 acres of forestland that is leased to over 200 hunting clubs.

The social value of life around a base camp is an incentive for many hunters to join a hunting club.

I saw firsthand the many benefits to hunters of belonging to a club that leased land for hunting. I also saw the advantages the landowner derived from leasing land to hunting clubs. It is a win-win proposition.

Many hunters join a hunting club in order to have an opportunity to participate in the management of land to produce quality of game to hunt.

These benefits are being realized throughout the United States, as public hunting lands are being reduced annually. Some public lands are crowded and downright dangerous; and on many, quality game management is minimal at best. Urbanization has taken up much of the "free" land many of us once hunted, and more acreage is threatened.

Therefore, hunters who are serious about their sport are forming clubs and leasing tracts of land from pulp and paper companies, timber companies, utility corporations, and petroleum and mining companies, as well as from farmers, ranchers, and some bank trust departments.

Here are some advantages of forming a hunting club and leasing land.

▶ You can hunt with other hunters you are compatible with and who share your long-term hunting goals.
▶ You have exclusive rights to hunt your lease.
▶ You can carry out a long-term wildlife management program and enjoy quality hunting for many years.
▶ By involving yourself in wildlife management practices on the property, you and your family or hunting partners can enjoy year-round activity on the lease. Many lessees find wildlife management activities to be as much fun as the hunt itself.
▶ Through a long-term lease, the next generation is assured a place to hunt.
▶ The members of many hunting clubs become fast friends and club members become part of an extended family. These hunters enjoy a camaraderie not found in other areas of life.
▶ A hunting lease can be much less expensive than a guided hunt or a hunt on distant public lands that require travel.

Equal advantages apply to the landowner who leases land to hunting clubs.

▶ Lessees usually develop a pride of ownership in the land, so they minimize trespassing, wildfires, dumping, illegal woodcutting, and other problems.
▶ The lessor knows who is on his land.
▶ The land can bring additional income without interfering with other income-producing sources, such as timber growth or oil pumping.
▶ Well-managed leases with a long-term, quality wildlife management program become more valuable to leasing in the future.

Despite their positive aspects, hunting leases can have trying moments as well. Finding a suitable tract of land can be very difficult for the hunter who has no experience dealing with land and who finds himself in an unfamiliar county or state.

Finding a hunting club a hunter is compatible with or forming a worry-free hunting club can be exasperating. Working through club decisions about purchasing insurance, whether to incorporate, and starting a wildlife management program can be a frustrating experience for the newcomer to leasing.

History

Actually, the concept of hunting clubs started in Europe many centuries ago when the wealthy owned the land and hunting was a social event. Clubs of the elite were organized to hunt fox, hunt driven grouse, and to hunt driven boar. To be a member of a hunting club was a status symbol.

In early American history, hunting clubs sprung up in New York, Wisconsin, Maryland, Virginia and other states, not because of the lack of hunting land but because hunters wanted to hunt the same land each year with a close group of friends. Many of these clubs were a combination of social, cultural, and sporting organizations. Some had as much interest in natural history as in hunting. In the early days, it was not unusual for a country tavern to be a club's base camp.

A number of hunting clubs became well known and someone had to die before a new member would be admitted. Clubs such as Deer Camp Erwin in Michigan, Buck Horn in Ohio, The Ridge Runners Company in Wisconsin, Ten Point Deer Club in Mississippi, and Cold Spring Hunt Club in Virginia became important parts of the region's history.

Private Land Access

Today hunting clubs are a way for the hunter of average means to have private lands upon which to hunt and to have a say in the wildlife management of the land. No longer can most people afford to purchase land for the sole purpose of hunting; however, a group of like-minded people can get together and pool their financial resources and lease a tract of land upon which to hunt. Whether leasing from a farmer, rancher, paper company, timber corporation or other large landowner, the hunt club may lease the recreational rights on the land for the entire year giving the lessees a great opportunity to hunt, fish, hike, camp, and shoot on the land. It is like owning a place in the country but at a fraction of the cost.

Belonging to a hunting club which has land exclusively for members to hunt on has many of the advantages of owning land.

By getting involved with the wildlife management on the property, the non-hunting months can be a lot of fun with time spent with friends cleaning out blinds, planting food plots, marking boundaries, cleaning up the clubhouse, scouting, etc.

The members
of many hunting clubs
become fast friends and
club members become part
of an extended family.

The Extended Family

The members of many hunting clubs become fast friends and the members become part of an extended family. Club activities such as family picnics, or cook-outs, fund-raisers, and kids days bring the members closer together and the club becomes an important social group for the members.

I have seen many clubs that were made up of strangers when they were first formed but after a few years they were like a large family whether hunting season was open or not.

A Nightmare or a Godsend?

When hunting clubs are formed correctly, managed for the good of all, and a strong positive relationship with the landowner is maintained, the clubs are usually a valuable asset for all the members. However, when a club is thrown together with little or no leadership, the club becomes a nightmare for all involved, especially the new member that didn't know what he was getting into.

The purpose of this book is to be a bible for anyone involved in a hunting club whether it is as a member, the landowner, a club officer, or someone who wants to start a hunting club. Over the years of being professionally involved with hundreds of hunting clubs I have seen the best and worst of clubs and made it my business to learn why the clubs were as they were. This book will give you the tools to have a good hunting club and help you avoid the pitfalls that make bad clubs.

Since the majority of the hunting leases of today are for the purpose of hunting deer, I have written many of the chapters in the language of deer leases. However, much of the same information will apply to the waterfowl, quail, pheasant, bear, elk, or wild turkey lease. So, do not despair when I say deer lease or deer club.

Let's get on with setting up the best hunting club in America.

FINDING LAND TO LEASE

A good contact for locating prime hunting country is a local county agent or other agricultural official.

George and John had what most deer hunters want—their very own hunting lease. They had found a tract of land, which had deer tracks on it, located the owner, and after writing him a check, shook hands to formalize their lease.

Since both George and John were bowhunters, they had driven from their homes the night before bow season opened and set up camp on their lease. Just after they got the tent up and the fire going, the owner drove up to inform them that he didn't allow camping or fires on his property. They would have to move their camp "right now." Tired and thoroughly disgusted, they struck camp, drove 20 miles into a small town, and checked into a local motel.

Things seemed better the next morning. They got into the woods, back on their lease before daylight and got their tree stands up in a large grove of white oaks. Their short night of moving camp and little sleep seemed worth it as they heard the first birds awaken and saw the first rays of the morning sun begin to show.

Suddenly they were almost jolted right out of their tree stands by two nearby shotgun blasts. Then there was a third right under them. As they climbed down from their tree stands, three squirrel hunters approached them. After a short conversation, the bowhunters learned that the squirrel hunters had a squirrel-hunting lease on the same tract of land. With this disappointment, the two deer leaseholders went home to wait for gun deer season. After all, they were really stalk hunters and it would be much better next month when the gun season opened. At least they wouldn't have to contend with squirrel hunters.

The opening weekend of gun deer season found George and John stalking quietly on their deer lease. Each had visions of slipping up on old mossy horns. Just after daybreak, they heard what sounded like the howling of wolves along the east border of their lease. Within a few minutes, 10 hounds ran between the two stalk hunters, hot on the trail of some unseen deer.

This pack of dogs had not been long in passing when they heard the music of another pack of hounds across the creek, which formed the northern boundary of their lease. It was very clear to them that the neighboring landowners weren't stalk hunters. George and John went home hoping that the "dog drive" hunters on the land surrounding their lease would soon grow tired of deer hunting and let the woods quiet down for stalk hunters.

While waiting for their next hunt, the two leaseholders sold three of their friends memberships in the lease. Since they were all good ole boys, nobody bothered to set up any rules.

The next Friday found all five of the lease members on the lease long before daylight. Some 15 minutes after good daylight, one of the new members got cold, built a fire and started shouting for John to come join him at the fire for a drink of "liquid sunshine." John had to climb up the ridge where he had been watching a spike trail a doe to get to the fire, quiet his friend, and put out the roaring bonfire.

Again, things got settled and the hunters were at peace with the outdoors. Suddenly there was a shot, then another, then another, then several more. One of the new members had gotten bored with the hunt and had started shooting into squirrel nests. As he walked through the woods enjoying the practice with his .30-06, he spotted a brown movement under a large oak in a pasture next to the south boundary. He sighted and fired just as the Hereford bull started to rise.

For the next six months, both George and John were in their attorney's office many times trying to straighten out their mess. This nightmare they called a lease almost caused them to swear off deer hunting.

If this deer-hunting lease sounds like a horror story, take heed, because it could happen to you. Every year many honorable, well-meaning hunters get involved in disappointing and poorly run hunting leases.

> Every year many honorable, well-meaning hunters get involved in disappointing and poorly run hunting leases.

Finding Your Lease

The first step in setting up a smooth-working hunting lease is to find a good tract of land to lease. Your search should begin in spring or early summer to give yourself plenty of time to find the right tract before the fall hunting season. Far too many hunters wait until a week or so before the season opens to begin their search. To their disappointment, they find all the good tracts have been taken.

Immediately following hunting season can be a good time to start looking. Many good leases are canceled then because there is no interest, a hunting club splits up, or lessees move out of the area.

First, you should determine the county in which you wish to locate your lease. Next, learn the habits and habitat of the deer, or other game of interest, in that area during hunting season. Habits, food choices, etc., change with the seasons and from area to area within the state. If you cannot recognize quality deer habitat, admit it and seek assistance. There are many government agencies in most counties with trained personnel who can help you learn to recognize good deer habitat. The USDA Natural Resources Conservation Service, Cooperative Extension Service, state game and fish agency, and the U.S. Forest Service are just a few that can help you get off on the right foot.

As you learn to recognize good deer habitat, sharpen up your skill of reading deer sign. In order to get a good deer lease, you will have to be able to read deer sign such as tracks, droppings, rubs, etc.

Once you are up-to-date on evaluating deer habitat and sign in your chosen county, obtain several copies of that county's road map.

Set up a series of meetings on a weekday with the following officials: The County Agent—He visits all the farms and knows something of the game population. In addition, he knows local landowners who may have a good tract of land for lease. The County Forester—He knows the woods; Natural Resources Conservation Service Representative—He is familiar with game management on farms and waterways; and the local Conservation Officer. If there is a timber or pulp and paper company in the county, visit their office, as many of these companies offer some excellent deer leases.

Rural mail carriers can be a good source of locating land to lease.

When you visit each of these contacts, go alone. They talk more openly to one sincere hunter than to a whole group asking many questions at once.

When visiting local people to search for your lease, be sure to dress as the local people dress. For several years I managed over 200 hunting leases and one of the quickest ways for a group to get a negative response when inquiring about lease land was to come into my office in full camouflage clothing, soaked in buck lure, and spitting tobacco juice in my secretary's trash can.

Be cautious not to overdo it from the other direction. Don't look for the land to lease in the boss's new Lincoln, as the lease price has a way of going up to pretentious lookers.

Most good hunting lands are in rural counties and the local people are much more apt to work with you if you look and act much like them.

As you visit each of the above-named contacts, have them mark on a county road map the areas they think have the best deer population. Also, write down the names and addresses of large landowners in the area. Use a separate map for each of these contacts. You will get thoughts that are more original by the use of separate maps.

After making your visits, compare the maps. Where there is an overlap in the officials' best-thought deer areas, you'll probably find the best deer hunting in the county.

Your next step will be to ride up and down the roads in the recommended area or areas of the county. As you get to know the area, establish some local contacts. The farmer on the side of the road, the rural mail carrier, and the crossroads store owners are all good people to ask about the local deer situation. Lead into the deer hunting questions slowly. Ask questions such as: "Are deer damaging crops?" or "Are deer a highway hazard?" or "Where do you see deer most often crossing the road?" Mark these areas on your road map.

Once you have several "hotspots" marked on your map, ride by them. Ask yourself this question: "Is it the right type of habitat?" If so, meet the landowner and discuss

Taking the time to visit landowners and prime hunting country is a good way to locate an outstanding lease.

the possibilities of leasing, subject to further investigation. Be friendly and don't rush.

Once you have found a willing landowner with a sizable tract of land carrying a good deer population, you will want to walk the land out thoroughly. Be sure of what you are getting. Get a wildlife biologist involved and ask the following questions, and if you don't get a satisfactory answer, beware.

What is the current carrying capacity of the tract? Find out how many deer the land will support. Is the deer population above or below that number? A local wildlife biologist can usually answer these questions in short order. If a local government biologist is unavailable, it is money well spent to pay a consulting wildlife biologist to visit the prospective lease tract. He can give you a professional opinion on the current game status and its potential for the lease.

Next, find out whether the tract is the right size for your purposes. If the deer population is one deer per 10 acres, for example, an individual wanting a personal lease may not need more than 100 acres. However, if the population is one deer per 40 acres, a group of five hunters may need to lease several hundred acres to give each of them a chance at a mature buck.

Financial restrictions may also dictate how large your tract should be. A 1,000-acre lease at $9 per acre can be a sizable annual payment for a small group of hunters. Match the size of the tract to the estimated game population, number of hunters to hunt the tract and the amount of money available for lease payments.

How well are the boundaries of the property marked? Well-marked boundaries can keep neighbors from wandering onto your lease and lessees from wandering onto their neighbor's. If the boundaries are not well marked, talk to the landowner about who will mark them. On a large tract, this is no small chore.

Often conservation officers and other wildlife officials know of land available that a hunting club could lease.

Is the landowner willing to let you carry out wildlife management practices such as clearing and planting food plots, doing prescribed burns and killing unantlered deer in cases of overpopulation? Will he be responsible for any of these practices?

On any lease tract, a biologist should draw up a wildlife management plan, and the parties involved should be in total agreement on the practices to be followed and who will be responsible for what. The clearing of land for food plots, the prescribed burning of selected land and the taking of unantlered deer can be very sensitive subjects to a landowner, and they need to be a part of the decision-making process. Is this understanding a part of your written lease?

Do you have exclusive hunting rights on the tract, or are your rights for only one species? A lease to different parties for each game species usually leads to trouble for everyone. The deer hunter who must share his woods with a squirrel hunter usually has his early-morning hunts disturbed several times during an over-lapping season.

Does the landowner retain rights for his family's hunting? This usually doesn't work well for lessees. Insist on total hunting rights.

How is hunting conducted on neighboring tracts? Hunters who lease land adjacent to a lease of dog-drive rabbit hunters usually wind up unhappy and feuding with the neighbors. Adjacent tracts should be hunted by methods compatible with your own. I have found that more leases are broken by conflicting neighbors than anything except internal conflicts among lessees.

You will probably want to lease your tract for a long time, so you need to know the landowner's long-range plans. Will the wooded part of the tract be cut for wood products? Will it be cleared for pasture? Are there silent plans for gas and oil drilling or strip mining? Make this part of the written lease.

Access to the land is important, especially during long periods of rain or snow. Who will be responsible for the maintenance of roads? A lease you can't get to or around on is almost useless.

Road maintenance can be very expensive, so have a clear understanding of who is responsible and when the work will be done. A landowner who agrees to the maintenance but performs only every other year may be unsatisfactory.

At the same time, agree on who will keep the gates repaired. Gates on roads leading into hood hunting leases keep others out; however, less scrupulous and jealous people often tear down these gates. In many areas, gate maintenance is a major chore.

Does the landowner agree with your hunting methods? Is it OK with him for you to use ATVs? Does he want only shotgun hunting, but you like to rifle hunt? Are you a bowhunter who likes to use a portable tree stand and he a timber grower who doesn't want any device used that skins the tree bark? The list could go on and on, but the bottom line is, talk with the landowner before committing to a lease. Be sure you agree.

Where will you stay when you hunt on the lease? Will the landowner allow you to camp, construct a base camp, use a campfire, or perhaps rent you a vacant tenant house on or near the property? If not, are motels or a public campground nearby?

Can you lease year-round recreational rights and will he permit you to build a small shooting range on the property?

Be sure you think of everything when you are talking with the landowner and keep notes for use in writing the details into your lease. I have seen a paper company lease land to hunters and then turn around and do a lot of prescribed burning during the hunting season. Fall burning burns up the browse and mast available to the deer. This same company once started a burn while the lease members were in their tree stands bowhunting. It is foolish to lease 2,000 acres and then have the owner burn it during hunting season. Be sure you understand and get in writing the long-range plans from the owner.

Once the landowner has answered these questions, determine the cost of the lease and the length of the lease. Before talking about the cost of the lease, check around the local area and learn what the going rate is for hunting leases. Be prepared to pay the going rate but know enough to avoid price gouging. The cost is up to you and the landowner; however, the length of the lease should be three to five years with an option to renew. A good tract of land properly managed for deer and leased to a sincere club grows in value. The older the lease, the more valuable it usually becomes to the members, so don't settle for one year.

It's nice to be able to trust others, but avoid the "I'm as good as my word" lease. A handshake won't do any good when you've paid several hundred dollars for a deer lease and arrive on opening morning to find that the land has been clear-cut. Once you reach a full agreement with the landowner, get the lease and all the particulars in writing. Make your lease a legal document. It will solve many potential problems in the future before they become problems.

> People with hunting land available for lease, often post their offerings in sporting goods and hardware stores.

THE WRITTEN LEASE

Responsibility for roads and gates should be negotiated by the hunting club.

I would like to have a dollar for every horror story I have heard where an oral agreement or a short written lease thrown together by a landowner and members of a hunting club established a hunting lease. A well-thought-out written lease reviewed by an attorney is worth its weight in gold as it solves many of the potential problems of a hunting club before they become problems.

The Appendix of this book has a sample hunting lease for your use. Since each state has different statutes, be sure you review this lease agreement with your attorney and have your attorney review your lease when it is completed and ready to sign. Other sample lease agreements are available from the Cooperative Extension Service in each state and, at this writing, on the Web at www.legaldocs.com.

Simply put, a hunting lease describes the agreements between the landowner and the hunting club members so that there are no misunderstandings about the rights being purchased. The following clauses are intended as a checklist of suggestions on the items of understanding usually found in a hunting lease.

Long-term land management goals and a schedule of timber harvesting dates should be spelled out in a hunting lease. A clear-cut, such as in the photo above, is an unpleasant surprise to find on your property a few weeks before hunting season.

These are taken from leases that have stood the test of time in many states.

▸ State the name(s) of the landowner, lessor, and the name of the hunting club who wishes to purchase the hunting rights, lessee.

▸ Give a legal description of the land being leased. A map of the property should be attached to the lease.

▸ Duration of the lease. State the term of years of the lease giving a specific starting date and termination date. If a right of renewal is given, spell it out.

▸ Reserve the right of either party to cancel the lease, stating causes, such as the violation of game laws, not living up to the terms of the lease, or a general out such as a cancellation in writing 90 days prior to the next annual payment.

▸ Amount and method of payments giving specific due dates. Some leases are based on acreage and some are based on animals taken. The method of calculation should be spelled out.

▸ Prevent lessee from subleasing property.

▸ A liability release that should be initialed by all members of the club or be on the same page as the signatures. An attorney should be involved on this clause as the requirements vary from state to state.

▸ Insurance requirements of landowner.

▸ Species to be hunted.

▸ Other recreational rights, or all recreational rights, such as varmint hunting, target shooting, fishing, hiking, and photography during nonhunting season.

▸ Special wildlife management requirements such as reporting game animals taken and special data gathering that may be required. Be specific.

▸ Clause for camping, campfire use, erecting camp structures, cutting firewood, RV parking, etc.

▸ Protection of fields, gates, livestock, trees, or structures.

- Description of who will maintain roads and/or bridges and when the work will be done.

- Clause dealing with wildfires.

- Clause dealing with the lessee abiding by all laws. Cancellation if violated.

- Establish no-hunting zones around job sites, livestock, and farm structures.

- Number of hunters permitted on property.

- Use of tree stands, nails in trees, etc.

- Lessor's ingress and egress rights.

- Lessee's right to develop food plots, trails, roads, etc.

- Restrictions of ATVs, four-wheel-drive vehicles and vehicles in general.

- Lessor's right to deny access to the leased property to any person with just cause.

- Special provisions such as specific days when no hunting is allowed; deadlines to remove decoys, blinds, campers, etc; hunting privileges for landowner or family; restrictions regarding the use of alcohol, disposal of animal parts.

- Signatures of all parties concerned, witnesses, and date.

Know what recreational rights you have and don't have when leasing a tract of land.

Whether or not you need to have the lease agreement recorded in official county records is a decision that you should leave up to your attorney. Most that I have been involved in were not.

Many pulp and paper companies, timber companies, and utility companies that lease their land for hunting have their own lease agreements. Most of these I have seen were well thought out and fair to both parties; however, it would be a good idea to have your attorney check out any lease you plan to sign.

An excellent booklet on hunting leases, entitled *The Texas Deer Lease*, is available for a small fee from Real Estate Center, Texas A&M University, College Station, TX 77843-2115.

...it is best to start out with friends of a like interest as the founding members...

ORGANIZING A HUNTING CLUB

Have you found a tract of land that you would like to lease for hunting but it's more than you can afford alone? You didn't like your old hunting club and would like to set up your own so it would be run right. You and your hunting buddies would like to organize a hunting club and find some land to lease. Whatever the reason, new hunting clubs are organized all the time and the good news is that if they are organized and managed correctly they stand a good chance of being around a long time.

Starting a hunting club is easy if the person doing the organizing is a strong leader and plans each step of the process. Some of the best clubs I have seen are small clubs with only four or five members. They had their organizational meeting around someone's dining room table. Getting the word out for workdays is easy. However, larger clubs are not that easy and require more organizational skills and effort.

Who and How Many Members

This is one of those chicken and egg questions. If you already have a tract of land selected, then the amount of dues money you need may dictate how many members you need. If you haven't already selected a tract of land, then you can get as many members as you want and find a tract of land large enough for the group.

Perhaps "Who" is more important than "how many." Anyone who has a serious interest in hunting the game for which the club is being organized, and who is

Prospective members of a hunting club should have the same interests and goals in wildlife management that should be reflected in the bylaws.

congenial with the other members, is a potential member. However, it is best to start out with friends of a like interest as the founding members and then slowly invite others to join after you are satisfied that their interest and intentions are the same as the founding group. Almost every hunting club goes through a weeding out process every now and then but you don't during the start-up if you can avoid it. Take your time and pick your members carefully.

The First Meeting

The first meeting is the most important meeting as this is usually when the officers are elected, club name chosen, bylaws adopted, fees set, and committees appointed. Make every attempt to get all prospective members to attend. Prepare meeting notices in the form of cards or letters and mail them to each person, inviting them to attend. Select a date and hour for the meeting that will be convenient for the majority of the prospective members. State the objectives and purposes of the club. If a tract of land has been selected, tell a little about the land. Also, serve refreshments and let it be known in the invitation.

Before the meeting, decide on a temporary chairman. He should be good on his feet in front of a group. He should call the meeting to order and get the proceedings under way promptly. He should state the purpose of the club, tell about the tract of land selected or what type of land the club will be searching. There is nothing like the possibility of an exclusive tract of land to hunt to generate excitement in a new club.

Next, the temporary chairman should open up the meeting for discussion. Then he will call for a vote to see if the group wants to form a hunting club. If so, then proceed with the actual formation of the club, which includes the election of officers and adoption of bylaws, selection of club name, and appointment of committees. Organize the fundamentals of the club at this first meeting and set plans in motion to lease that special tract of land. If land has already been selected, it may be possible to set the initiation fee and dues at that time. How much time has been spent preparing for this meeting will determine as to how much you can cover and not have the meeting go on for too long.

I have been to several organizational meetings where the club was formed and operational by the time the first meeting was over; however, these meetings were well planned.

Election of Officers

Hunting club officers may be president, vice president, secretary, treasurer, hunt master and safety officer. Acting together, they can constitute the Executive Committee. It is important that the officers be carefully selected to be good organizers, know how to maintain records, and have strong leadership skills. Particular care should be given to the election of the president since his contribution to the club goes beyond formalized duties such as presiding at meetings. He will meet with the landowner of the lease land, set standards for the club, and solve member disputes.

Club Name

Club names suggesting the sport of hunting are most commonly used but a name relating to some feature of the hunting land is a close second. Examples of club names include Bear Creek, Five Shot, Big Buck, Ten Point, Paradise Hill, and Hickory Ridge. Choose the shortest name that will best represent your group.

Initiation Fee and Dues

When considering the amount of initiation fee and annual club dues, the first thing to determine is what expenditures will be called for by the club's programs in a given year; and second, how large a membership your club will have. Expenses will include land rent, food plot seeds, fertilizer, boundary signs, possible clubhouse renovations, and utilities. The list could go on depending upon the goals of the club. Once you have made a realistic expenditure evaluation and a determination of the members, then the dues can be set accordingly. Be careful not to set them too high or too low. Decide upon a fee that will get the job done but will not be a burden to the club members.

Committees

A committee may be appointed to search for land to lease, get a wildlife management plan written for land already leased, or to design a base camp. By using committees, the president can get club members involved with the club, thus keeping interest high while getting vital jobs done.

Arrange for the Next Meeting

Before adjourning the first meeting, a time, place, and date should be set for the next meeting. Plan the date for your next meeting so that each of your committees has time to gather the proper material and information, so that definite activities can be acted upon by the membership. Be careful not to extend the time so far into the future that the members lose interest.

Hunting Club Bylaws

A sample copy of hunting club bylaws is given in the Appendix of this book. Bylaws should govern the day-to-day operation of the club. Adapt the bylaws to local conditions that affect the club, its relationship with landowners, and its use of wildlife resources. Avoid overly burdensome bylaws. Many new clubs create too many bylaws and are unable to enforce them. Add bylaws as needed. Hunting club bylaws should address management of the lease property, safety, guest policy, hunting rules and regulations, operational committees, disciplinary procedures, and member-landowner relationships.

To Incorporate or Not

Your hunting club is engaged in an activity that has potential liability to third parties or to members; so there may be advantages to incorporation, especially if the club owns land or other valuable property.

A cooperation has such advantages as more freedom from personal liability than other forms of organization, continuity of existence, convenient method for members to join their resources and efforts together, and a background of legal and administrative precedents to help it operate properly.

A cooperation is a legal entity. All legal proceedings can be carried on by the cooperation as a body. It has a well-defined legal status with all rights spelled out by statute. The cooperation is founded on a legal structure, which makes clear what the organization can and cannot do. Members are less likely to be sued as individuals for damages, unless gross negligence or utter disregard for public society is present. Then only guilty members may be sued.

On the other hand, incorporation is usually not a requirement of most landowners leasing land and the advantages of incorporation are by no means conclusive. If the club has adequate liability insurance for the protection of its members and landowner, and wishes to operate on a relatively informal basis, the club may elect to operate as an unincorporated organization, as thousands of other clubs do. In fact, most of the hunting clubs I have worked with are unincorporated and have had no problems. When organizing a club you should seek the advice of an attorney concerning the need for incorporation.

The first meeting
of a hunting club can
determine the success or
failure of the club.

INSURANCE

A hunting club's insurance policy should take into consideration all type of potential liabilities such as a member's use of ATVs.

It was the beginning of the perfect weekend. Ray had invited his new neighbor Jim to his hunting club for a weekend of deer hunting. While Jim was new to deer hunting, he was excited about spending the weekend hunting with Ray.

They arrived at the club cabin just before midnight on Friday night and unloaded Ray's two ATVs to be ready for leaving before daylight the next morning. Jim wasn't much help with the ATVs, as he had never ridden one before. Ray assured him that the unit he had brought for Jim to use was easy to ride, as it was fully automatic.

The following morning the two neighbors enjoyed a big camp breakfast and went out into the cold to start the ATVs for the ride to their stands. Ray gave Jim a few pointers about the ATV he was to ride and off they rode in the darkness.

Accidents can and will happen even in the best managed hunt club. Every club should have a comprehensive general liability insurance policy to protect its members and their investment.

At a fork in the road Ray gave Jim directions as to where his stand was located and they agreed to meet at the fork at 11:00 to ride back to camp for lunch. With that, they each disappeared into the darkness. Ray really liked his neighbor and was glad he wanted to learn more about deer hunting. In fact, Ray was working to get him a membership into the hunting club.

Later that morning Ray arrived at the fork in the road. He couldn't wait to tell Jim about the nine-pointer he saw but never got a shot at. He waited until 11:20 and when Jim never showed up Ray smiled thinking his neighbor just may be struggling with a big buck.

Ray cranked up his ATV and started down the road to where Jim was hunting. Rounding a bend in the road, his heart sank as he saw the ATV Jim was riding upside down in a deep ditch. He raced to the ditch to find Jim folded up under the machine barely able to talk. He had multiple fractures, a fractured spine, a concussion, and several deep cuts. He had been there since early morning and was near death.

Fortunately, Jim survived after a long hospital stay, several surgeries, and lots of physical therapy. He missed months of work and his medical expenses amounted to almost $500,000.

Who would pay all the medical bills? Who would support Jim's family while he was out of work? Who was responsible for the accident since Jim had no ATV riding instruction and it wasn't his unit? Would the club and Ray be sued? The list of unanswered questions went on and on. Fortunately, for Ray and his club, they had a general liability insurance policy that provided coverage for the club if they were found legally responsible for this accident. The same policy covered Ray as well.

Accidents of all types happen on hunting clubs every hunting season. Shooting, tree stand falls, ATV wrecks, fire, and falls in general are among the most common accidents that cause deaths or injuries on hunting leases. During the years I managed hunting leases, I saw these and other unusual accidents many times and usually the club couldn't believe it had happened on their lease. Fortunately, we required every club to carry a general liability insurance policy and name the company I worked for as an additional insured in the policy.

Even simple camp chores can be the potential source of litigation if proper insurance has not been purchased by the hunting club.

Every hunting club needs general liability insurance for the protection of the club as well as for each of its members. In addition, for a small additional fee the landowner should be named as an additional insured, most lessors require it.

According to Dr. Ed Wilson, a hunting club insurance expert with the Davis-Garvin Agency, writing in *Quality Whitetails* magazine, "simplified, liability insurance is designed to provide coverage for hunting clubs and their members for acts which they could be held legally responsible. Thus, the insurance is designed to lessen the risk associated with occurrences caused by a negligent act of the hunting club or members and guests. Clearly, all hunters and landowners should be aware of the risks they are taking by not having adequate liability insurance. It's simply not worth risking all of your personal assets or your family's security for unfortunate accidents or the acts of members of your hunting club."

What Coverage Should You Have?

The coverage package that is most recommended by the insurance agents contacted at this writing is one which has the following:

- $1 million per occurrence general liability coverage
- $2 million general aggregate
- $100,000 fire legal liability
- Member-to-member coverage
- Guest liability coverage
- Liability coverage for firearms, tree stands, ATVs, mobile equipment, limited watercraft, hunting dogs, and more

Policies of this type are available through organizations such as the Quality Deer Management Association and the Forest Landowners Association. In the Appendix of this book, I list a number of good sources of hunting club insurance.

How Much Does a Policy Cost?

The cost of a policy such as the one described above will vary from underwriter to underwriter and will vary depending upon the number of acres in your hunting lease. However, I shopped out hunting club insurance as I was writing this chapter, based on 1,000 acres, and the annual cost ranged from $222 to $360. A small price to pay for the peace of mind that comes from knowing you are protected in a case like Ray was in at the beginning of this chapter.

"The club's rules must spell out what is acceptable at the club and what is not…[and] the rules have to be enforced."

DRAWING UP CLUB RULES

Rules are important if a hunting club is to offer a quality experience for its members, says Bernard Austin of Metairie, Louisiana. Austin is president of the Warrior Hunting Club and has served as president of the club for several terms. He gives the club's rules credit for the low turnover in members. "The club's rules must spell out what is acceptable at the club and what is not. Next, the rules have to be enforced," he says.

Elements of the Rules

Harvest. Warrior Hunting Club is primarily a deer-hunting club, so the rules begin by listing what deer can be harvested. Its members participate in a quality deer management program, and a number of doe tags must be filled each season. The rules explain how each member is responsible for keeping harvest data.

Guests. Club property is relatively small, just 1,000 acres, and the club lodge sleeps 10. Therefore, rules regarding guests must be explicit. Each member is allowed only four guests per season, at $30 per visit. No guest may visit the club more than twice during a season. Nonhunting guests must follow the same rules. The host is responsible for the guest and must be at the lodge as long as the guest is there.

Safety. A number of rules apply to safety. Each hunter must place a tack on a map, located in the lodge great room, showing where he is going to be hunting. This serves several purposes. If he doesn't return, other members know where

Hunting club rules should include off-season use of the club property.

Club rules should cover all aspects of use by the guests of club members. Each member should be required to be responsible for any quest he invites to the club.

to start the search. In addition, it keeps other members from hunting near the area. No member is allowed at the lodge alone. "We once had a member pass out, and if he had been alone he wouldn't have made it," Austin recalls. An orange line painted on trees a few hundred yards from the lodge reminds hunters to unload fire-arms at that point.

Consequences. "Our rules spell out what happens if a member or guest doesn't follow the rules," says Austin. All new members are on probation for one year. If a member is expelled from the club, there is no refund on his dues. "The rules must have teeth, or they aren't of much use," he says.

Miscellaneous. Because the club has a lodge to maintain, there are rules for keeping the building clean and in good condition.

A hunting club is just like any other group in a civilized society. If the members draw up a good set of rules and follow them, everyone will enjoy the hunting experience. It works at the Warrior Hunting Club.

This is just one of thousands of examples of how clubs use rules to keep the club run smoothly. Every situation is different and every club should tailor their rules to their goals and desires for good hunting.

Tips to Consider When Drawing Up Rules

Violation of Game & Fish Laws. It should be a club rule that no game & fish law violation will be tolerated and that the matter will be turned over to a conservation officer immediately. For this and many other reasons, invite the local conservation officer out to the club property and show him around. Inform him that your club has a zero tolerance toward game law violations and he will be called if there should ever be one.

Game to Be Harvested. Be specific about what game is to be harvested and when. Unless a club has a lot of land, it is best that only one game species be hunted during a season. Deer hunters don't want squirrel hunters walking under their stand shooting rimfire rifles. In addition, a hunter who has been trying to wait out an old buck for several days doesn't want a group of raccoon-hunting members running in his area all night. What about if a coyote runs through your area just at daybreak, does your club permit you to shoot legal varmints? This all needs to be spelled out in the rules.

Size and Sex of Game. If your club is in a quality deer management program there will be size restrictions on bucks and each member will be expected to help in the doe harvest. Some clubs do not permit the taking of bucks until each member has taken his share of does. Your rules should spell out how the deer harvest is to be conducted and what data the member must pull from each deer taken. Good recordkeeping is a must.

Hunting Methods. Club rules should state how members are expected to hunt, check-in rules and checkout rules, area restrictions, and any other expectations of the hunters. Many clubs are dedicated to still or stalk hunting and do not want man-drives. If so, state it in the rules. If you must stay on your stand or in your hunting area during certain hours, state it. Most hunters will hunt according to the rules if they know what is expected.

ATV Use. I once was a member of a club that permitted ATV use without any rules. Soon we had some hot rod members that were cutting "donuts" in all the food plots and running almost nonstop on the club roads all day. It quickly became an issue and almost destroyed the club. ATVs are a valuable tool to have in a hunting camp but their use must be regulated and the rules must stress common sense and courtesy for their use.

Spelling out who can hunt what game and when is an important part of a hunting club's rules. As an example, some members hunting squirrels during deer season may drive members away from the club.

Litter. There should be rules concerning litter. Bring out of the field all that you took out with you, and this includes blinds. I have gone to duck and deer blinds that were akin to going to a garbage dump. Keep the woods and blinds clean. Also, address where deer entrails, hides, feet, and other waste parts are to be taken. This can be a major health hazard on clubs and it can attract every stray dog in the region, which can have a negative effect on hunting. Plan on how to handle waste parts of animals before the season opens and put the solution into the rules.

Club rules should be very specific about how the base camp is to be cared for and exactly who is responsible for cleanup.

Dog Problems. During the years I worked with hunting leases I saw, on several occasions, people almost get into a shootout over the handling of dogs that strayed onto the club property, usually chasing deer. Free-ranging dogs whether chasing deer, hanging around camp, or strolling in front of your stand just before dark are not welcome guests. Develop, with some imput from the local conservation officer, how club members should handle the problem. Put it in the rules.

Camp Rules. If your club has a lodge, camp house or other type of structure, there needs to be a separate set of rules and we will discuss this later in this book. If you have a camping area, skinning shed, or general gathering area, some rules should be drawn up on how to keep the area clean. Spell out if firewood cutting is permitted or if it must be hauled in. State fire rules and what to do if there is a wildfire.

Rules Should Stress Safety. Have a well-thought out set of safety rules. Be strict with firearms especially in camp. If the club has a shooting range, have a separate set of rules posted at the range for range use.

Have Specific Rules for Alcohol Use. Some clubs forbid the use of alcohol on the club, others do not permit the use of alcohol until the hunt and all shooting activities are over for the day, and others say when you take a drink, gun handling is over for that day. We all know that alcohol and guns don't mix; so set your rules to have a safe hunt and camp.

Workday Requirements. Every club must have workdays to plant food plots, fertilize native food plants, clear roads, clean camps, etc. Rules are required to accomplish this and we will discuss this in a later chapter of this book.

We could go on for pages about rules but each club must set their own rules and enforce them.

Handling Rule Violations

The best clubs have a zero tolerance to those who break the more important rules one time or are a repeat violator of the minor rules. The quicker you weed out those people who choose to break the rules, the better the club environment will be.

Most clubs requires that a grievance or complaint against a club member must be reported to an officer or board member. Then a hearing is usually held so that all parties involved may speak their mind. The club bylaws should have a clause that permits the reviewing board to dismiss a member immediately if he is found guilty of not following the club rules. If it is truly a nonserious over-sight, put the offender on probation; but if he is clearly one that cannot play by the rules, do the club a favor and ask him to leave.

In many cases, I have seen a strong, but fair, president dismiss a serious rule breaker the same day the offense occurred. Most agree the sooner you can solve these types of problems, the better. Think about these types of problems when you write your club's bylaws.

If the members draw up a good set
of rules and follow them, everyone will
enjoy the hunting experience.

Joining a hunting club
is a lot like getting married...
you hope to stay together
for the long term.

JOINING A HUNTING CLUB

Jerry Dawson had just moved to a new town to become regional manager of his company. None of the people at work hunted and Dawson was making enough now that he could afford to join a hunting club. It was his dream to become a part of a great group of guys who had their own place to hunt. He looked forward to getting involved in the wildlife management on the club and someday when his son was old enough have their own club on which to hunt together.

Dawson asked around about hunting clubs but all he heard about were full with a waiting list. One Sunday just before deer season opened, he saw a short ad in the local newspaper, "wanted hunting club member" with a phone number. Excited, Dawson called the number several times before he got an answer. The voice on the other end told Dawson he had a group of trophy hunters and they leased 2,500 acres in the southern part of the county. There was plenty of deer and if he wanted to join the group he should send a check for $750 as quickly as possible as there were several hunters wanting to join. Dawson asked to visit the lease but the response was no one would be there until opening morning. Dawson committed and got instructions as to where to send the check and how to reach the lease.

Participating in a hunt with a prospective hunting club is a good way to see if this is a good club you want to join.

Opening morning at 4:30 a.m., Dawson drove up to the old tenant house that served as the club's base camp. As he walked into the dimly lit room, he was shocked at what he saw. Most members had a beer in their hand and all were talking at the same time. They were organizing a man-drive and those with AK-47s would be the drivers. "We get in more shooting when we are the drivers," a burly man in military camo told Dawson.

Someone offered the new member a beer and asked him how much ammo he brought. The club "president" assigned Dawson a pickup truck to get in the back of and soon a number of pickup trucks were speeding along logging roads in the cold dawn air.

That morning Dawson spent hidden behind a large log in fear of his life. The deer drive was a shooting and hollering contest. As the disorganized line of club members swung past Dawson, a doe passed by him and two shots were fired at her. Then a staggering driver came over to Dawson cursing the fact he missed every deer he had tried to shoot and wondered if Dawson had an extra "brew."

Dawson couldn't wait to get back to his truck so he could go home. His $750 was gone and he was considering taking up golf.

Locating Hunting Clubs

Dawson made many mistakes when he decided to join a hunting club. Don't make the same mistakes. First, start your search as early in the year as possible. Give yourself plenty of time to study the clubs you find which have membership openings.

One of the best places to start your search is to call the local conservation officer or county agricultural agent. Both have contact with hunting clubs as well as with landowners who lease land to clubs. If they recommend a club, it would be worth contacting.

Many hunting clubs recruit new members via posting an ad for members in local sporting goods stores.

Another good source is the local sporting goods store or gun shop. While you are talking to these people watch the local newspaper. Often under the heading of "hunting and fishing," you will find ads seeking members for hunting clubs.

Regardless of where you hear of a club with an opening, start your interview process with caution. While it may be a new club trying to fill its membership rolls for the first time, or just a club with an unexpected vacancy, be cautious as most good clubs have a waiting list for membership openings. A club having to search for members may have problems. Keep your ears and eyes open.

A good way to get to know about the members of a hunting club and whether or not you would like to be a member of this group is to help them during a work weekend.

Look Carefully at Prospective Clubs

Joining a hunting club is a lot like getting married, you join up with the best of intensions, and you hope to stay together for the long term. Approach it with the same caution.

Before beginning your search, determine what you really want. What game is most important to you, what hunting methods do you enjoy most, do you want a lease that offers more than just one species of hunting, perhaps a place to shoot and hike during the nonhunting season?

Determine how much are you willing to spend for the initiation fee and an annual membership fee.

Once you have found a club or clubs to interview, set up a lunch with the president and **find out the answers to these questions before you take the next step:**

- Is the lease a year-round lease with all recreational rights or just for certain species or seasons. Is there a small shooting range on the property you can use?

- Find out how many members are in the club and how many acres it leases. From whom do they lease and what are the terms of the lease.

- What is the price of the membership and how much is the initiation fee. Does this include everything, or will the members be expected to pay for more add-ons later. Does your membership assure you a vote in how the club is run?

- What is the club's guest policy? Is there an additional fee for a guest?

- Is the club and its members insured and, if so, for how much?

Joining the right hunting club can guarantee a quality hunting experience …

▶ How are grievances settled?

▶ Does the club have a written wildlife management plan supervised by a wildlife biologist? Do they regulate their hunting according to the plan? Is data kept on the game taken? If the lease is to produce quality deer hunting for many years, these questions must have a "yes" answer. If not, the membership should be considered a short-term investment.

▶ Ask for a copy of the property map, club's bylaws, harvest records, and rules. Study them carefully. Make sure you agree with the rules and that safety is stressed. Is the quality of game taken what you would be happy with?

▶ Find out who is in the club and see if you can get a membership roster. A few calls to other members can tell you a lot about the club. See if you can determine that they abide by game laws, how they hunt, what nights at camp are like, and how they feel about wildlife management on the lease. Take the time to find out who you will be hunting with.

Visit the Club

▶ If possible, visit the club lease while the members are there. The best way to do this and to really get to know them is to volunteer for a workday. Under these circumstances, you can get to know them much better and they you. Take a map and go over the property, look at their roads, food plots, stands, camp, etc. Be honest with yourself, do you like what you see?

▶ Attend a club meeting if possible and see how the business side of the club is run.

▶ In the end, the decision is yours. However, if you have gone through the process outlined above, you will be able to make an informed decision.

Joining the right hunting club can assure you of a quality hunting experience, provided it is done correctly. It can be a great way to avoid the crowds and to hunt with friends who hunt the way you enjoy.

GUEST POLICIES

A guest should know what is expected of him when staying at the club's base camp. Food and bedding arrangements should be made in advance of a guest's arrival.

Everybody likes to hunt with a hunting buddy. It's just more fun. Because we all know that, most hunting clubs have a guest policy that allows the members to bring friends and family on hunts. On the surface, that sounds very good but it is often a privilege that brings down clubs, makes members turn on one another, and creates problems for all concerned. I have seen uninformed guests abuse poorly written rules in many ways.

⯈ Often a member will keep bringing the same guest repeatedly. Soon it becomes apparent to the other members that the guest is simply avoiding the cost of initiation fee and dues, but using the lease as much as the members. I have noticed these types are never around as a volunteer on workdays.

⯈ A common problem is the guest who doesn't fit in. He drinks too much, eats everyone else's food, is loud and obnoxious, never helps with camp chores or he knows how the club could be better run. One visit is too much, but these types usually keep coming back.

‣ Clubs that have liberal family guest privileges sometimes find their hunts are actually a mini-family reunion for one of the members. They can dominate a hunt or weekend. The paying members feel they are intruding. Then there is the member who brings his kids, who really wishes they weren't there, and depends upon the camp to help baby-sit them for the weekend.

‣ More than once I have seen clubs break up due to a member bringing his girlfriend to the camp for a weekend of romance. The other members are there to enjoy a hunt and camp life.

‣ Clubs with no guest limit will see the member who brings two or three guests, usually "very important people," and suddenly the property is crowded and many times these guests get the better hunting areas. I see this happen most often during the rut.

The list could go on for pages but the point is guest privileges can ruin an otherwise good hunting club quickly. Since the guest problems are usually family, close friends, neighbors, or "the boss," the member who brings them is offended when it's brought to his attention and an internal war is started.

Stop the Problem before It Becomes a Problem

Since we all have friends and family we would like to share a hunt with, a guest privilege is important for most clubs. (I do know of some hunting clubs that do not permit guests.) To keep the guest privileges from getting out of hand and to be fair to all members of the club, it should be well thought out, with all members having input, and should be in writing. It should be a part of the club's bylaws, and a method of enforcement spelled out. Copies should be posted on the club bulletin board and each member should have a copy. It is most important that a new prospective member receives a copy before he becomes a member. Some clubs require a guest be given a copy to sign before he visits the club. He then knows that his visit is a privilege and knows beforehand what the club expects of him.

Guest policies should spell out exactly how a hunting club guest should conduct himself on the club property. Did this hunting club guest know he was not suppose to drive his ATV on food plots?

The written guest rules with strong, swift, enforcement will solve most visitor problems before they become problems.

What to Include in a Guest Policy

While every club has special conditions and ideas about guests, here are some pointers to be considered when writing a new guest policy or rewriting one that may not be working in the best interest of the members:

▶ Charge a fee for each day a guest hunts on the club property. It costs just as much for a guest to kill a buck or gobbler as it does for a member. The guest usually doesn't help on workdays and doesn't pay dues. At this writing, the clubs I contacted charge from $25 to $70 per day for a guest. Two clubs I contacted charge an additional trophy fee if the guest takes a buck or gobbler. Remember, that buck or gobbler could have been taken by a hardworking club member. It should be the host club member's responsibility to pay the guest fee when the visit is made.

▶ Determine the number of guests the property can support in one day. What if every member showed up with a guest? The size of your property and overnight accommodations will dictate how many people, safely and comfortably, can hunt on the property. Don't have a guest policy so liberal that the property is overhunted or the clubhouse is overflowing. You may want to have a per day guest limit with advance notice being required. The number of guests the lease can accommodate may change from squirrel season to deer season to spring gobbler season.

▶ Since some members may want to bring a guest every time they come to hunt, you should limit the number of guest visits each member can have. Most clubs limit each member with three to five guest days per season. That varies with length of seasons and population of game. However, it is wise to set a limit.

Hunting guest policies should always require that the host member of the club be fully responsible for the conduct of his guest.

Since we all have friends and family we would like to share a hunt with, a guest privilege is important for most clubs.

▷ Be sure to limit the visits a specific individual can make to the club. I have seen people visit a club regularly, enjoy good hunting, and avoid the membership payments and workdays. Limiting an individual to two visits per hunting season will help stop freeloading.

▷ Have a family member policy. Keep it to immediate family members. Again, keep the size of the accommodations and property in mind when setting up this policy. A large hunting family can tax the facility. This is a touchy subject with some people so get all members involved in the decision. Also, keep in mind at some point children of members reach an age when they should purchase a membership.

▷ Have a youth policy even for family members. Many clubs require that a youth can only hunt after he has successfully passed a hunter education program. Consider having hunting youth hunt with an adult until they reach 16 years of age or so. That is a judgment call you need to make carefully. Nonhunting youth should be required to be with an adult at all times.

▷ Guests who eat and sleep at the club camp need food and a bed. Set up a policy to provide for this. When there are 10 bunks and 10 members spending the night, where are the two guests going to sleep? What about food and who is going to cook it? Guests are guests and should be treated with respect but, when they show up with no food and no cooking skills, who is going to take care of them. I have seen some serious problems in nice hunting club base camps when a host brought in guests and didn't plan on how to feed them or where they were going to sleep.

▷ Make sure all guests have a set of club rules and understand them before going out to hunt. Guests need to know what is expected of them, what the game harvest rules are, and how the hunts are conducted. Good rules usually spell this out.

▷ Consider having a guest ID card and a temporary guest pass for display on a vehicle or an ATV. This keeps confusion to a minimum with other members who may not know "this stranger" is a guest of the club.

▶ Require all guests to sign a liability waiver. This can help the club if a guest should be involved in an accident. A sample is found in the Appendix of this book.

▶ The guest and his actions will be the responsibility of the host member.

Enforcement

Guest policy and written rules are so that everyone hunting on the club lease will enjoy himself or herself. Most of the times enforcement of the rules is unnecessary; however, when the rules are broken, swift enforcement is necessary before the situation grows. Many clubs give enforcement power to any officer or board member. If it is a minor infraction, then a short talk with the host member is usually all that is needed. However, if it is a major violation of the rules, then discipline of the host member and dismissal of the guest are required.

The discipline of the host member should be in accordance with the club rules, and the guest should be removed from the welcome list. While this is an oversimplification, each case must be reviewed and handled based on the circumstances. Sometimes guests do things beyond the host's control and you can't blame the host member. Other times the host member is knowingly breaking the rules and the guest is simply doing as he is told. Listen to the facts and be fair in the action taken.

Guests should be expected to learn the boundaries of the hunt club property and to know the hunting methods of the club.

It's a little slice of freedom,
an escape from the "real world"
and a place we all look forward
to returning to year after year.

MANAGING THE CLUBHOUSE

The heart of most hunting clubs is the "camp," be it a large lodge, converted school bus, mobile home, skinning shed, large tent, old tenant house, or log cabin. Throughout the country "camp" is a different structure to different clubs but what is the same is that it is where the meals are cooked, hunting stories told, hunters sleep, and traditions made. It's a little slice of freedom, an escape from the "real world" and a place we all look forward to returning to year after year.

Coming back to this special place is a lot less fun if when we return we find someone left a window open and your sleeping bag is soaked, several dishes of leftovers were left in the refrigerator several weeks ago, someone didn't turn the water off at the well and the pipes are all frozen, or the place looks like a fraternity party was held in the great room and it will take half a day to clean the place up. I have seen these and countless other acts of inconsideration at hunting club camps and it's a shame because with a little effort the camp could always be a reasonably clean, organized place to hang your hunting hat.

Small clubs usually have fewer problems with keeping the camp orderly than do large clubs. In small clubs a simple Standard Operating Procedure (SOP) posted in the kitchen will usually get the job done. In larger clubs

Hunting club base camps range from tent camps to farmhouses to repossessed mobile homes. This Iowa hunting club base camp is a restored farmhouse that offers all the comforts of home.

appointing a camp master to make sure the SOP is followed can be a good idea, especially if the camp is a nice lodge or cabin where the club has a financial investment.

My camp is a log cabin where eight of us hunt. It does not have running water or electricity. An outhouse is our toilet. We have designed an SOP that not only includes how to operate in the cabin but we incorporated the grounds care, shooting range, and outhouse in the SOP. Much of the SOP deals with how to leave the cabin when shutting down after a hunting trip. In 11 years of heavy hunting use, we have had no problems. A sample of this SOP is in the Appendix of this book.

Clubs that have a camp master usually select a member who likes to cook and spends a lot of time at the camp. It seems that those who like to cook have a knack for knowing how to keep a camp clean and they take pride in the kitchen, a source of many camp problems.

Base camp rules should include policies on how to leave the camp when everyone goes home.

A lot of hunting club camps I have visited have the kitchen cabinets divided into small sections with each member getting a section for the storage of his kitchen supplies. The space in the refrigerator(s) is usually equally divided, and some members who come less often use an ice chest to store their perishables.

Garbage builds up fast in an active hunting club and where it can be correctly disposed is something a club should check out as soon as they lease the land. The camp master should appoint someone daily to take care of the garbage.

It should be up to each member spending the night to keep the sleeping quarters clean and in a reasonable orderly condition. Trashy camps become nasty, unhealthy, rat infested, and often a fire hazard.

Another area that can become a mess is the skinning shed or area where game is cleaned. Those who use it should be responsible for cleaning it and hauling off the waste after each use. The club rules should spell this out and those who want to leave a mess for others should find another club.

It is always a pleasure to be in a club where each member takes pride in the camp and without any organizational meetings or a camp boss; everyone knows what to do and pitches in to keep the camp clean and orderly. Members who have hunted together for years work as a team and the job of tending camp is easy and fun for all.

These are examples of the many types of base camps found at American hunting clubs.

Some members value
the club's shooting range as
much as the hunting. It's also
a good recruitment tool for
getting new members.

THE SHOOTING RANGE

H unting clubs that have developed a shooting range on their lease find that it becomes one of the most popular features of the club. A good friend of mine, Vann Cleveland, is the treasurer of Pine Hill Hunting Club in Alabama. Vann tells me that when his club built a small shooting range on their property the members started showing more interest in their marksmanship, particularly shot placement on deer. The new range gave the members a more efficient place to sight-in rifles and hunting handguns, and during the off-season, they had a nice range to visit for a weekend of shooting. It's just one more amenity that makes the hunting club membership valuable.

The hunting club shooting range may be a permanent structure such as this one or a simple temporary shooting bench safely located near the base camp.

Many of the clubs I have worked with, or been a member of, have built a small shooting range on the property, usually near the camp, and it becomes a real asset to the club. Some members value the club's shooting range as much as the hunting. It's also a good recruitment tool for getting new members.

Hunting clubs on a tight budget can invest in a portable shooting bench and set up a range without breaking the budget.

Getting Permission First

The first rule to building a small permanent shooting range on the lease property is to get written permission of the landowner. I have found the best way to do this is to have a definite plan before you approach the landowner. As likely as not, when you say shooting range, he is going to think commercial range with numerous shooting positions and dozens of shooters shooting at the same time. The plan will ease these fears.

Go to the landowner with a safe location in mind. Show him in person, or on a map, the suggested location. If a berm must be pushed up tell him. Show him the shooting bench to be built, a plan for the shed if you are going to build a cover over the bench, a plan or sketch of the target stand, and a set of the range rules. Emphasize that the range is designed for safety, only one person will be shooting at a time, it will be kept clean and will be for members only.

Most of the time landowners welcome a well-run, safe small range rather than having a club sight-in guns whenever, however, wherever. If he agrees, get it in writing.

Site Selection

Look for a site near your base camp but far enough away from the camp and any other neighbors so that the noise from the shooting won't disturb anyone. The site should avoid an east-west orientation to keep the sun out of shooters' eyes, morning or evening. It should be fairly level for the distance to the farthest targets. Most club ranges are 100 yards. Pick a site that has a steep hill for an impact area or get a bulldozer to push up a high berm. Be sure it is in an area where you can post it with warning signs to keep wanderers out of the area. Signs are available from Signs by John Voss. *(See Appendix F-6.)*

To check the chosen site, go to the location you want to erect the shooting bench and set up a portable shooting bench. Next, measure down to the most distant target. Set up a target. Then, check out the arrangement every hour or so for a day. If it is satisfactory the entire day, go with it.

Laying Out and Building the Range

There is plenty of help on range layout, shooting bench construction, and target stand construction from the National Rifle Association and the National Shooting Sports Foundation. *(See Appendix F-7.)* The actual lay of a small shooting range is simple. Select a site for the shooting bench. You will want a site that is level and usually dry. There should be room for the bench, a bulletin board, gun rack and seats for spectators. If a covered shed is to be built, make sure there is room for it.

Next, measure down to the location of the target stand and make sure it lines up with the shooting bench and the safety backstop. Clear out any brush that may obstruct shooting.

Construction of the range and the posting of the warning signs can usually be done in one workday if several of the club members stay on it.

The club range is usually more popular than most members think at first; so build the facility so that several members can be there safely at one time and give serious consideration to putting a covered shed over the shooting bench, bulletin board, and benches where those waiting to shoot can sit out of the sun or rain.

I only mention one shooting bench because for most clubs that works well and it is easier to keep the shooting situation safe. However, if more shooting benches are desired, it is easy to include them.

The bulletin board serves a multitude of purposes including the posting of the range rules, club rules, interesting shooting information, etc.

Pattern Board Range for Shotguns

Since many clubs offer wild turkey hunting, as well as other waterfowl and upland game hunting, the interest in including a pattern board range next to the rifle/

Clubs with a permanent shooting range report that members' shooting skills in the field improve due to more frequent shooting practice.

handgun range grows. It is easy to build one and takes little space. All you need is a level area for 40 yards with a hill or berm at the end to use as a backstop to stop pellets.

Start by building the pattern board just in front of the hill or berm. Place two 8' x 4" x 4" pressure-treated posts in the ground 2 feet deep. They need to be 36" apart, measured outside to outside. Anchor the posts in the ground by pouring concrete in the holes. Use a level to make sure the posts are perfectly vertical. After the posts have settled, nail a pressure-treated board 36" x 2" x 4" across the top of the post. Come down 40" from the top and nail a second 36" x 2"x 4." These two 2" x 4" 's are simply cross bracing. Finally nail or screw a 36" x 36" sheet of 1/2-inch plywood or waferboard. You will staple your targets upon this pattern board. It will last for many shots and is easy to replace as needed.

With the pattern board built, use a tape measure to determine 30- and 40-yard shooting stations. At each point dig into the ground a hole deep enough to place a 24" x 24" x 2" concrete walk pad such as found at building supply dealers or home improvement stores. Don't set shooting stations any closer to the pattern board since there is some danger of shots bouncing off the pattern board. If you wish to test your loads farther than the traditional 40 yards, you can add a shooting station at 50 yards, and I have seen some waterfowl hunters have one at 60 yards.

Having a shooting range as a part of the hunting club base camp offers the members an opportunity for sighting-in rifles.

If most of your pattern work is done at 40 yards, you can put in a post, waist high, at that station and build a 12" x 12" platform on it to place shot shells, etc.

The pattern board range can be developed right beside the club's rifle range. If you do this, it is a good idea to put the 40-yard shooting station in line with the shooting bench. Also, make it a rule that rifle/ handgun shooters will not shoot at the pattern board.

WILDLIFE MANAGEMENT PLAN

One of the main reasons most people join a hunting club is to have a good place to hunt. Some leases have a healthy game population when a club leases them and some may be marginal. Those that have a good game population will only stay that way for a short while without sound management, and those with marginal populations will only get worse if they are hunted without management.

A good example is a 1,500-acre lease tract I worked with in South Carolina. A farmer owned the land. It was mostly in a pine-hardwood mix forest. While the farmer did little to improve the habitat, the tract had a fair deer population that still had not reached the carrying capacity of the land. Wanting to make an income on the property, the farmer leased the hunting rights to a hunting club. The club knew nothing and cared less about deer management. They wanted

Wildlife biologists are available for the asking to help hunting clubs design a wildlife management plan for their club property.

to hunt as much as they could and success to them was how many deer each member took during the long South Carolina season. Many of the members quit their jobs when deer season opened and hunted almost every day, and possibly many nights.

After three hunting seasons, they complained to the landowner that there weren't any large bucks on the lease and the deer population wasn't what they expected. The club was killing a lot less deer than they were three years ago. To avoid having to listen to constant whining the farmer canceled the lease.

Word got out that the land was available and soon a small club of six hunters leased it. They were about as interested in deer management as in hunting and knew they had a long way to go if they were to get this property back to its deer potential.

A long-term wildlife management plan, properly followed by a hunting club, will result in satisfaction for the members.

They hired me to help them come up with a written wildlife management plan for the property. This group was a pleasant change, in attitude, from the former lessees and the landowner agreed to do the planting of food plots for the club.

We took several months in writing the plan and started with improving the habitat. The plan called for prescribed burning, the creation of food plots, food plots to be planted for both warm season plants and cold season plants, fertilization of native food plants, posting of the land and cooperation of the local conservation officer to help stop illegal hunting and trespassing.

We discovered that the deer population on the tract was very low and no mature bucks could be found. Knowing this, we designed the plan to put the club on a quality deer management program and slowly began to take doe in a very selective manner. It took five years of patience and annual adjustments to the plan, but the club developed into a deer hunter's paradise. The club members took almost no deer the first couple of years but now they take wall hangers and their children have a great place to start their hunting careers.

How to Get a Wildlife Management Plan Written for Your Club

If your hunting club leases land from a timber company, paper products company, bank trust department or utility company, chances are good the company has a wildlife biologist running the hunting lease program and you either are working with a plan or can get one simply by requesting one. However, if you lease from an individual or smaller company, you may not have the services of a biologist and will have to find one on your own.

Often hunting club members get as much out of participating in the wildlife management of the club as they do participating in the hunting.

It is surprising to many hunting clubs as to how easy it is to get a professional wildlife biologist to write you a wildlife management plan and help you follow the plan to improve the hunting on your lease. Every state game and fish agency offers the free services of their wildlife biologists to anyone who asks. I emphasize, you must ask. State wildlife biologists are very busy professionals and rarely do they have time to go out and seek clubs to write wildlife management plans. However, when a club calls their office and asks for help it is usually forthcoming. *(See Appendix F-2 for contact information.)*

Each state has wildlife management planning assistance available through the USDA Natural Resource and Conservation Service. By requesting help through their district conservationist, you can get a wildlife management plan under way. *(See Appendix F-2 for contact information.)*

Wildlife management planning assistance is available through the Cooperative Extension Service. A request for help through the local agricultural county agent will get the ball rolling. *(See Appendix F-2 for contact information.)*

As I said earlier, this assistance is free and even with heavy schedules these wildlife professionals are always glad to help an interested club together a management plan.

What to Expect in a Wildlife Management Plan

A wildlife management plan is exactly what it says, a plan to help you manage the wildlife on your club's property to achieve a reasonable goal you set. In the case of deer, you will have to decide if you want more deer, or do you want to maintain the deer population at about the same level or have trophy bucks. Simple questions, but there is much more to it than most hunters think.

The plan will include an aerial photo of the club property or a map of some type. The first section of the plan will establish what your long-term goals are in terms of what you realistically want in the way of wildlife resources. For this part of the planning process, the club should agree as to what they want. Part of the membership can't want the property to have lots of deer, average or less bucks, as their priority while the other members want trophy class bucks to hunt. This leads to personal conflicts and conflicts in hunting management.

... wildlife professionals are always glad to help an interested club put together a well thought out management plan.

The second section of the plan will state the present population of game, the condition of the habitat and some history, if known, of past harvest data, hunting management, and wildlife management. Knowing this, the wildlife professional will then draw up a plan that will include habitat management needed to reach the goal, harvest recommendations, data keeping system necessary to monitor the management success, and other recommendations he thinks may be necessary to reach the goals.

Many of the habitat recommendations are written up in the plan and the areas are marked on the aerial photo or map. It makes it easy for the club to carry out the habitat improvements.

This is a long-term plan but one that must be studied annually to make adjustments especially in the harvest recommendations. It can take years to see a major improvement but it is well worth the wait.

Wildlife management plans are as individual as biologists but the above gives you a good idea as to what your plan will look like. Many of the plans of today are done with the help of computers and sections such as harvest data and evaluation are computer generated.

If you are in your hunting club to enjoy quality hunting, both for yourself and your children, you and your club should obtain and follow a wildlife management plan.

NWTF Offers Wildlife Management Assistance

The National Wild Turkey Federation (NWTF), through its Woodlands Private Lands Hunting Club Program, offers a lot of benefits to wildlife and the hunting clubs that adopt the program. Among the benefits to clubs are information on developing wildlife management plans, recommendations for wildlife management, discounts on seeds and seed mixes, and a free copy of *Get in the Game*, an excellent wildlife management CD which gives guidance for land management, food plots, mapping and data collection needs. Each hunting club which signs up for the program is eligible to participate in the NWTF's Wild Turkey Woodlands Hunting Clubs Awards Program.

QUALITY DEER MANAGEMENT

A rapidly growing number of deer hunting clubs are now opting to put their land into a quality deer management (QDM) program. QDM is a philosophy where land managers have the common goal of producing healthy deer herds with balanced adult sex ratios and age structures. This program promotes the harvesting of female deer in appropriate numbers to maintain herds within the carrying capacity of the land and social constraints while protecting young bucks. Clubs in this program usually set a minimum antler size on bucks to be harvested, such as no bucks less than eight points and the antler spread one inch or more outside the ears. This allows more bucks to reach maturity. In addition, they take a prescribed number of female deer each year. The fewer does results in the bucks having to work harder to find a receptive doe. Due to the intensity of rutting activities such as scraping, rubbing, and buck fighting, this increases hunter success and the quality of bucks taken by hunters goes up dramatically.

Letting young age-class bucks live is a basic principle to quality deer management.

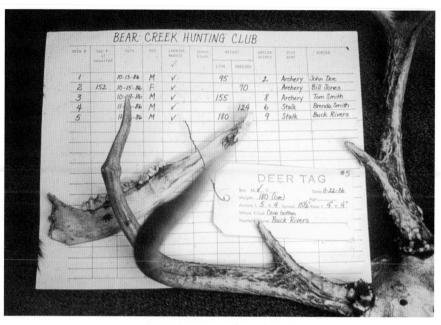

Accurate record-keeping of harvested bucks is necessary for a wildlife biologist to monitor a quality deer management program for a hunting club.

Hunting clubs that implement quality deer management programs find that the long-term benefits outweigh the setback of a restricted harvest.

QDM is summed up best by deer management professional Dr. David Guynn who says, "QDM is first and foremost an attitude, a means of self-expression. The hunter views a deer not as just a resource for recreation and food, but as a part of nature to which he or she belongs. A self-imposed restriction to take an antler-less deer while allowing young antlered bucks to pass provides the hunter with opportunities to study deer, learn their behaviors, and sharpen hunting skills. Deer hunting is the experience of giving to as well as taking from the deer."

There is so much interest in QDM today that an excellent organization called the Quality Deer Management Association, QDMA *(see Appendix F-1 for contact information)*, has been formed and is one of the fastest growing deer management organizations in the United States. All hunting club members who are interested in QDM should be a member of this nonprofit organization. It is a one-stop source of up-to-date information on QDM.

To go into the details of QDM in one chapter of this book would be wishful thinking. It is an interesting and complex subject on which books have been written.

If your club wants to go into a QDM program, contact your local state wildlife biologist and get him to write you a wildlife management plan to achieve this. I will caution you that it takes a lot of education to get all club members to be skilled enough to judge harvestable bucks and patience enough to pass up smaller bucks. They must also be willing to take the recommended number of female deer and learn how to recognize fawn bucks so that they aren't killed as does. The QDMA has much information and educational tools to help make this job easy and fun for the entire club.

Quality Deer Management Cooperatives

As you begin to learn more about QDM you will hear that, due to the travel patterns of deer, it takes large tracts of land to conduct a successful QDM program. This is discouraging news to members of small acreage clubs. Fret not, there is good news!

It is true that it takes tracts of land 2,000 acres and larger to successfully have a QDM program. However, several smaller contiguous tracts can join in a like-management program and form what is called a Quality Deer Management Cooperative. It works. There are now more than 100 co-ops in Texas and new ones are being organized throughout the country.

According to the QDMA, "by forming a cooperative, members gain the management advantages of a larger landowner. Cooperatives are voluntary affiliations and in no way entitle neighboring hunters access to your property or diminish the landowner's control. They are simply collections of landowners and hunters that establish and abide by agreed upon deer management guidelines to enable improved management over a larger area."

A long-term quality deer management program on a hunt club's property can result in trophy class bucks being harvested. The club, which has this reputation, will never find it difficult to find new members.

Here are the basic steps to organizing a QDM co-op:

▶ Contact your local wildlife biologist and ask him to help you organize a QDM co-op.

▶ Call the QDMA and ask them to supply you with detailed information on forming a QDM co-op.

▶ Contact your landowner and explain the co-op concept and ask him to help you form a co-op with your club property being part of the co-op. Most landowners are glad to participate once they realize it doesn't change anything other than improve the deer herd in the area.

▶ Identify the landowners of properties adjacent to your club and along with your landowner invite them to a meeting to discuss the possibility of forming a QDM co-op.

▶ At the meeting, if all landowners and clubs agree, simple bylaws are passed and co-op officers are selected. Next, the landowners sign a simple, not legally binding, agreement that states that all involved have the same deer management goals and will follow a co-op deer management plan and make all harvest data available to the local wildlife biologist. *(See Sample Cooperative Agreement, Appendix D.)*

With the land your club leases in a QDM co-op, you will know that the other clubs or hunters on the adjoining land are striving to manage their deer as you are. In addition, you will know that the little eight-pointer you passed up won't get shot on the neighbor's land.

Balancing the number of does to the number of bucks for a hunting club will be spelled out in the quality deer management long-term goals.

MAKING WORKDAYS WORK

A hunting club president once told me that everyone in his club is a good member as long as there is an open season, but let the seasons close and he had trouble getting anyone to do the many chores it takes to manage the land lease. "Say workday to my club members and many of them run," he added. It seems that this is a common problem with many clubs and it can lead to fights among club members and to clubs falling apart and losing their lease.

Well-organized workdays are often fun and productive.

Fortunately, a growing number of clubs have members that have discovered the fun and fellowship that can be had while spending weekends working on the hunting lease. In fact, many clubs now report that the workdays are popular events at their clubs and the members really enjoy carrying out game management practices, such as planting food plots, prescribe burning, aging deer jaws, calculating the harvest data, etc. Others enjoy learning new skills and the satisfaction that comes with doing physical work all day out in the woods.

The success of any hunting club, which has land and a base camp, will be determined by the willingness of all members to share the work load with a good attitude. That means when workdays are set, all attend and really work.

It Starts at the Top

Getting club members to show up and actually work on workdays requires that the club officers lead the way. I once saw a club that was organized by a man that appointed himself as the club's president. He would set workdays on their lease, assign duties to the members, but never show up to help do the work. This club lasted only one deer season. Having only a few members doing all the work on the lease and everyone else showing up to hunt is guaranteed failure for a club. If the leaders lead by example, it is much easier to get the others to get involved in workdays.

Have a Must-Attend Rule

Most successful hunting clubs have it in their bylaws that attending a set number of workdays are a must. Deer clubs usually have from eight to ten workdays per year. Each day may be from six to twelve hours long depending upon the work load. Usually the club's bylaws states that the member must attend at least four of these workdays. Some clubs state if you do not attend the minimum number of workdays, you are expelled from the club. Other clubs allow the member to pay a fine, usually $50 at this writing, if they miss a scheduled workday. This must be paid before hunting.

Many members are willing to put in extra days working on a hunting club when the goals of the club are clearly spelled out and everyone does his fair share of the work. When all members of a hunting club pitch in on workdays, a lot of improvements can be made on the club property in a short period of time. Club members should be notified well in advance of workdays, and when they arrive, the day should be planned with clear goals stated.

A hunt club member fills a seeder on the back of an ATV to sow a feed plot during a club workday. Well-organized club workdays can be enjoyable outdoor events for members

Having a fine for missed workdays works well for those members who have jobs that require weekend working, such as firemen and law enforcement officers.

Plan Workdays Carefully

Always announce workdays a month in advance as this gives members the opportunity to schedule the time away from home. Short notices of workdays usually lead to poorly attended workdays.

Know exactly what needs to be done on the property and assign work duties to match the skills of the members. A member with welding skills may be assigned to repair the iron gates to the property; farmers with farm equipment may work the food plots; members with chain saws may clear roads of fallen timber; carpentry and plumbing skills may be needed to repair the clubhouse. The list could go on but members are more efficient if they are assigned chores that match their skills. If they want to learn new skills such as soil testing food plots or constructing blinds, assign them to a work party that has the skills and can teach them without slowing down the job.

Have a master plan for the workday with a leader for each chore to be completed.

Make It Fun

I always enjoy working with a hunting club on their workdays when the group has a good attitude and the day is fun. Most clubs have cookouts as a part of a work-day weekend. Good food and fellowship are popular forms of motivation. Many club members want to learn more about wildlife management and workdays can be made a learning experience while getting a lot of work done. It is always more exciting to take a buck off a food plot you planted.

Working on workday chores is a good way to get to know all the club's members and to learn more about the lay of the club's property. You may be on a team that is marking the clubs boundary. Doing that you will probably see parts of the property you have never seen before. You may also find deer sign and a great place to hunt. Every time you work on the property, you are going to learn more about the land and the animals found there.

Know exactly what
needs to be done on the
property and assign
work duties
to match the skills of
the members.

Many club members tell me they enjoy going to the club property on their own time to do chores. Often they will take family members to help and make it a fun day in the outdoors. One club member I know takes his two teenage children to his hunt club several times each summer to fertilize native plant species deer like. It has created some excellent deer habitat. Moreover, the man and his kids love doing this as much as they do hunting. The club should keep a list posted (where members can see it) of small chores individual members can do on their own time.

A List of Hunting Lease Chores

While the chores of each hunting club will differ, here is a list of chores that most deer hunting clubs must do each year:

- Repair gates to public roads
- Clear fallen limbs and trees from interior roads
- Clean out road drains
- Clean up camp and do repairs
- Cut firewood
- Clean out and repair blinds
- Check stands for safety and repair
- Soil test food plots
- Break, lime, fertilize, and plant food plots
- Establish salt licks where legal
- Fertilize native plants such as smilax, honeysuckle, oak trees
- Mark boundary with posted signs
- Clean and repair shooting range
- Mark trails to blinds and stands
- Put exclusion cages in food plots
- Clean and equip the skinning shed

Well-run workdays can pull a club together and make the club a team, giving them the pride of ownership in the club and its property.

A hunter cautiously approaches his fallen quarry, a fine ten-point buck, one of the ultimate benefits of careful management and well-spent workdays. The willingness of all members to share the work load will assure both an excellent place to hunt and quality game.

BOUNDARY LINE MARKING

Well-marked
boundaries keep
club members on
the property and
keep neighbors
from straying onto
the club property.

The old saying that a well-marked boundary, property line, keeps "good neighbors" good has a lot of merit. Many major disagreements between hunting clubs and their neighbors result from boundary disputes along unmarked or poorly marked lines. Well-marked property lines can keep honest mistakes from becoming serious misunderstandings, and will notify less scrupulous individuals of your desire for no trespassing. In addition, well-marked lines make prosecuting trespassers much easier. Even though your state may not have good trespass laws, the clearly posted property line can be a good measure to prevent one of your hunting club members from straying onto an adjoining property not leased to your club.

Marking Property Lines

The first rule to follow when planning on marking your hunting club property lines is to have the landowner's permission. Many lessors such as paper companies, timber companies, bank trust departments, and utility companies want lessees to mark boundaries with signs the company furnishes. Others want to have approval of the size, wording, and material the signs are made of. Still other lessors want to mark the exterior lines themselves and let the club mark subdivided interior lines. Know your lessor's policy before you start marking lines.

Assuming your hunting clubs lessor grants you permission to mark the club's boundaries, have him approve the signs or method of marking you want to use. This should be in the written lease agreement. It can be discouraging to spend a weekend nailing up 300 posted signs to have the lessor tell you he doesn't like the wording on them and to take them all down.

Once you have permission to mark the boundary, get a current survey to use as a guide when marking the boundary. Have marking crews supervised by club members who are familiar with running survey lines and finding survey points such as corners. A member of the marking crew who is skilled with a compass can speed the process up considerably.

Permanent Line

If your lease is for a long term, several years, you may want to mark the boundary with signs or paint so that it will be marked for years, with only an annual check for fallen marked trees being required.

Many companies prefer paint because it is quick to mark. If the correct paint is used, it lasts for years. Many hunting clubs do not like to use paint, as the adjoining hunters may not know what the painted line means and stray over onto the property. In addition, the painted line does not warn potential trespassers to stay out of the property.

A variety of commercial boundary marking signs are available and care should be given both to what the sign says and to the projected life of the sign.

However, if paint is to be used, be sure to check with the lessors to see what color they prefer. Many companies use only one color to mark their property lines and you will want to stay with their color. Also, see how they prefer corners to be marked and how trees running along the line are to be marked. You would be surprised as to how many unique ways you can paint a tree on a property line.

Once you know the painting technique, go to a forestry supply store and purchase paint made specifically for marking boundary lines. Not just any exterior house paint will work. When marking trees along the line, the surface of each tree should be carefully prepared with a machete or hatchet. Remove only the loose bark from the area to be painted. Don't cut into the tree or you will damage it. You are to remove only loose bark. Paint an area on each side of the tree so the line can be seen from all sides. A band painted around the tree works well for property lines.

A three-man crew can paint lines quickly once they get organized. Have one member as the navigator, keeping the crew on the property line. A second member will select trees at the proper interval, within sight of the painted trees on either side, and remove the loose bark. The third member will paint the tree.

The most popular method of permanently marking property lines is the use of signs. Signs not only mark the boundary lines but they can warn trespassers they aren't welcome and, if the name of the hunting club is on the sign, a neighbor who needs to get permission to trail a hit deer will know who he needs to contact.

There are signs commercially made for posting hunting property. You can purchase them made of paper, plastic coated paper, plastic, and metal. Before selecting a material, decide what you want your sign to say. Don't invite trouble. Avoid signs, that offend the neighbors or present the reader with a challenge. I have known cases where offensive signs lead to clubhouses being burned down. Think how your sign is going to come across to the reader and don't issue a challenge to vandalize. I have found that the words "POSTED KEEP OUT" work about as well as any threat.

Aluminum nails should always be used for putting up signs when marking boundaries; they assure safety for forestry workers using saws when harvesting trees.

You may want to have the name of your club and/or a phone number printed on the signs so that those wishing to contact the club will know how. They may want to obtain permission to look for a hit deer, want to join the club, or report a problem.

The color of the signs is important as you don't want them to blend in with the trees during the hunting season. Pick a color that stands out and post the signs can be easily seen. If they blend in, they do little good.

Over the years, I have tried many sign materials. The only ones I have found that last for long periods, years, are those that are made from heavy plastic, treated to resist sun damage, and aluminum signs painted with paint that will resist sun damage.

A two-man crew can mark a boundary with signs. One member to navigate and one to nail signs to trees.

The signs should be placed on trees as high as one can comfortably secure them. Select live trees as dead trees will fall and the line will have a gap in the marking. Signs should be placed close enough so that anyone crossing the line at any point can see a sign. Thick cover will require more signs than open woods. A rule of thumb is to purchase 30 signs for each mile of line to be marked.

When putting up boundary signs, be sure to use wide headed two-inch aluminum nails. Aluminum nails wont damage saws or injure workers when the trees are cut. In addition, they last as long as the signs last.

Don't hammer the nail all the way into the tree. Remember the tree is going to continue growing so you need to leave at least a half inch of nail exposed for tree growth. Nails that are hammered all the way to the head into the tree will hold the sign next to the expanding tree and the expansion will pull the sign off the tree.

Clubs that have a lease for only a hunting season may want to consider paper or thin plastic signs as they cost less. There are some thin plastic posted signs that come on a roll of 200 and are torn off as needed. In addition, for short-term boundary marking, forestry supply stores offer plastic surveyor's tape that has the words "boundary line" on it. One man can tie the tape on trees around the clubs boundary in a short period of time.

Having a well-marked property line around your hunting lease will not stop the criminal trespasser but it will keep honest people honest and make prosecuting the criminal trespasser much easier.

Well-marked property lines can keep honest mistakes from becoming serious misunderstandings …

Special interest hunting clubs can be organized to provide for a wide variety of hunting interests.

SPECIAL INTEREST CLUBS

This book was written from the deer hunting club prospective simply because there are more deer hunting clubs that lease land than any other hunting interest. This is not to say that deer hunting clubs are more important or more interesting, far from it. I have had the pleasure of being a guest and belonging to clubs that specialized in many other species of hunt. They were just as interested in wildlife management and in running a good club for the benefit of every member. There are clubs for hunting waterfowl, quail, pheasants, grouse, squirrels, wild turkey, bear, elk, rabbit, and wild hog. As I was working on this book, I was on a hunt in Canada and had the opportunity to visit a moose hunting club. There can be a club for any hunting interest.

Waterfowl hunting clubs are almost as numerous as deer hunting clubs.

Each type of hunting club has special conditions of the hunt, wildlife management, and facilities that must be taken into consideration when writing bylaws and club rules. Wild turkey hunting clubs require more land per hunter and hunting zones must be set up to keep hunters from hunting the same gobbler. Upland game clubs such as for quail, grouse, pheasants, and even squirrel often need facilities and rules for dogs. Waterfowl clubs have blinds and pits that require special rules. Using this book as a guideline, most of the principles and documents discussed here can be modified to fit almost any type of hunting club.

It is recommended that whatever species of game animal you lease or buy land on which to hunt, you set up a wildlife management plan the club can use to guide it in making harvest decisions and land management plans. Even the prolific rabbit can be overhunted and without sound habitat management, it can disappear quickly.

Unique Hunting Club

A unique special interest hunting club has been formed in Alabama that is certain to be followed in the future. The Disabled Sportsmen of Alabama partnered with the Lakeshore Foundation of Birmingham, Alabama, to create a hunting club for disabled hunters. The foundation leases land from a land development company. The hunting land features wheelchair accessible facilities such as a lodge, blinds, and rest rooms. For more information on this unique opportunity, call the Lakeshore Foundation at 205-868-2065.

> Some of the earliest hunting clubs were formal organizations intended for fox hunting.

MAPPING THE PROPERTY

Perhaps the most valuable tools a hunting club has are its topographical maps and aerial photographs of the club property. Maps of the property are used to plan the wildlife management programs exercised on the property. They are what keep members and guests on the right property and are used for planning hunts and coordinating where everyone will be hunting. Maps are used by members and guests for navigating in the woods and not getting lost. In addition, maps are used to relive great moments on the lease.

Aerial photographs play an important role in planning the wildlife management for a hunting club property.

Not long ago topographical maps and aerial photos were hard to get and often expensive. However, today there are many sources of maps and they are available at a reasonable cost. Most clubs need several topographical maps and aerial photos in order to make the club's property management program and hunts go smoothly. Investing in a good map/aerial photo supply is a wise investment for any club, whether their specialty is deer hunting or duck hunting. Here is a recommended list of maps/aerial photos.

Poster-Size Map of Club Property for Base Camp: At some convenient, weatherproof site at the club base camp, a large topographical map and an aerial photo need to be posted for hunt planning and coordinating where members and guests are on a daily basis. This map and aerial photo should have the club's property boundary marked on it as well as roads, permanent blinds, buildings and any other permanent features. These maps should have a clear plastic covering over them to protect them and so that a grease pencil can be used to mark on them.

Maps and Aerial Photographs for Wildlife Management Plan: Most wildlife biologists will want both an aerial photo and a topographic map of the hunting club's property upon which to record many recommended practices included in the club's master wildlife management plan. The club should keep a duplicate of these maps and photos so they can keep up with the location of recommended management practices.

In addition, while we are discussing management plans and maps, your wildlife management planner may want to get a copy of the soils map of your club's property. These can be obtained from the USDA Natural Resources Conservation Service agent in the county in which your hunting club property is located.

Small Topo and/or Aerial Photo for Members'/ Guests' Use: Every person hunting on the hunt club should have a small map of the property for use in hunt planning, navigation, and to make sure he does not wander off the property. Small maps and/or aerial photos can be downloaded from the Web or printed from a mapping software program.

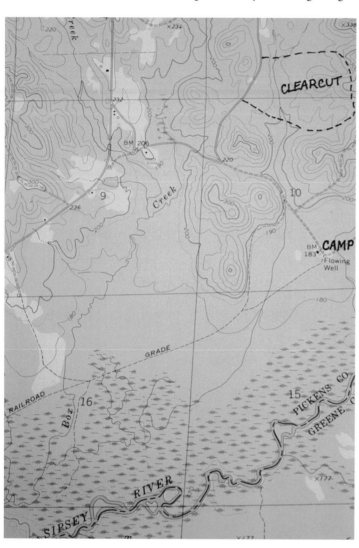

Topographical maps are vital tools for managing hunting clubs.

Obtaining Maps and Aerial Photos

As I stated earlier there are now many good sources of topo maps and aerial photos and more coming on the scene annually. Government agencies and private companies offer maps at reasonable prices. Here are some sources where your club can get its maps and aerial photos.

On-line Sources: One of the best free on-line sources of small topo maps and aerial photos is Terra Server, www.terraserver.microsoft.com. At this site, you can download a topo map or aerial photo of your hunting club property and the surrounding area. You select the general location of your club property, then zoom in, and download your map or photo. Once you have the image on your computer, you can print copies or modify the map with a graphics software program. You can also order high-quality aerial photos on the Web from Earth-Photo Imaging and Mapping, www.earth-photo.gov. Another on-line source for topo maps and aerial photos is myTopo, www.mytopo.com.

Government Sources: Topo maps and aerial photos are available from the U.S. Geological Survey (USGS), www.usgs.com. Their topo maps are often for sale at bookstores, outdoor outfitter stores and regional USGS map stores.

Hunters use an aerial map to relive the adventures of their morning hunt.

On a local level, aerial photos are available from the USDA Natural Resources Conservation Service or the Farm Service Agency located in the county in which your hunting club property is located.

Software Programs That Allow You to Make Custom Maps: The software program I have used for several years is Terrain Navigator offered by Maptech, www.maptech.com/topo. With this program, you can print your own version of a USGS topo map; record property lines, and trails, stand sites; and mark and measure distance with just a click of a mouse. You can also view maps in four zoom levels, with path elevation and line-of-sight profiling, along with an extensive place finder. You can automatically load stand sites or routes to stands into your GPS.

Another topo mapping software program is available from DeLORME, www. delorme.com/quads. This program gives you a 3-D look at your hunt club property.

Aerial photographs are useful
for hunt planning and can be easily
downloaded from the Internet.

RECRUITING NEW MEMBERS

T he Fox Hill Hunting Club lost one of its most valuable members when his employer transferred him out of state. That left the 20-member club one member short. Hunting season was rapidly approaching as was the lease payment, so the club was desperate to find a new member. With the club's approval, the secretary took out an ad in the local paper.

After running two weeks, the ad resulted in three people interested in joining. The club president decided to offer the membership to the first person who answered the ad; after all, he sounded nice on the phone and was obviously interested in deer hunting.

It is often during the after-hours around the base camp that prospective new members realize the value of joining a hunting club.

As soon as the prospective member got the invitation, he sent in his dues payment and became a member. Two weeks later, a workday was held at the lease and the new member didn't show up. Six weeks later, the night before the deer season, the new member showed up at the hunt camp with his brother-in-law, a guest, and they both were drunk. It was a touchy situation but they soon went to sleep, the brother-in-law in another member's bunk. Opening morning, the two slept in while the rest of the club went hunting. Midmorning, they woke up and cooked a large breakfast, other members' food, and got into their truck and rode around the lease. They rode by several members' stands and ran deer out of several food plots.

At noon, the club president had received complaints about the new member from all the other members. He approached the new member and explained the club's rules, which covered such behavior, and told him this was his only warning. The new member apologized and promised it would never happen again.

The following Friday night, the new member showed up at the hunt camp with a cheap-looking young woman and announced that she was his guest. He was also overheard telling her that they were going to ride around to all the food plots and see if they could shine on any deer eyes.

That was it. The club president asked them to leave and when the new member refused, a scuffle ensued and the new member and his guest finally left. The next Monday, the club president was charged with assault and battery. The new member had become a nightmare.

Prospective new club members should be given the opportunity to visit the hunting club property and to review the club's bylaws and rules.

This is a true story. Recruiting new members into a hunting club is usually a good experience but caution is advised when it is a prospective member no one knows. Remember, you are going to have to live with this member for a long time so take the time to recruit someone with like interests and goals.

I know of another club that thought it was a neat idea to raffle off a one-year membership. They raised a lot of money selling tickets but got one of the area's worst poachers as a member. It took them most of the hunting season to run him off, plus it took the services of an attorney. Several of the members quit because of the new member's actions. It took the club several years to get back to normal. In the meantime, the hunt club cabin burned mysteriously.

Know Who You Want for a Member

Every hunting club has its unique personality. Yours will also. Before you start recruiting new members, know what kind of person you want for a member. If you have an established club that is enjoyable, you will want someone who is a lot like the other members. You will want someone who has the same wildlife management and land management values as the club. A new member who wants to shoot young bucks shouldn't be in a quality deer management club.

Look for a new member whose hunting methods are the same as the other club members'. If your club members are stand hunters, then they are not going to be very tolerant of a new member who rides his ATV nonstop looking for deer.

When considering new members, determine what skills they may bring to the club that would be useful. I know many clubs that give special consideration to prospective members, all other things being equal, who are farmers, wildlife professionals, construction workers, law enforcement, and accountants. These people bring valuable skills to the club that help maintain the camp, manage the land and improvements, and run the club efficiently.

Don'ts

▶ Do not assume that anyone who can come up with the money to join your club will be a good member.

▶ Do not think family members "think alike" and will automatically be a good member.

▶ Do not think your club will never need new members.

▶ Do not think a bad member won't destroy a club.

▶ Do not trust one member to judge a prospective member. Have several members help with the decision to offer him a membership.

▶ Do not sign up a new member who has not read the club's bylaws and rules and agreed to live by them and like it.

▶ Do not fail to check with the prospective new member's past hunting club, if you find that he has been a member of one.

Anthony Paternostro of Carriere, Mississippi, has organized about as many hunting clubs as anyone I have ever worked with. Anthony advises to start a recruiting program within the club. He advises to use external recruiting efforts such as newspaper ads as only a last resort.

Recruit from Within

At the first sign that there may be a membership becoming open, let the members know. Ask them if they have friends who might be interested in joining the club. Chances are if the club is well run and has a good reputation, there will people wanting to join. If the property you have is a good place to hunt, that alone is incentive for friends of members to want to join.

Recruiting a new hunting club member can often be the beginning of a lifetime friendship.

A prospective new member should be given the opportunity to hunt with the club as a guest. You get to learn more about him and he about the club.

While the members are a great source for new member recruiting, Anthony warns not to accept them in until you meet them and if possible have them participate in a workday. Workdays will tell you a lot about a prospective member. A little time spent screening and getting to know a prospective new member is time well spent and can help avoid a bad situation.

Invite Guests to Join

The second best source of new members are those who have visited the club as guests. These are generally persons that the club has been around and chances are good they may have been there several times and members have gotten to know them. The person knows you and you both know what to expect. I have found that guests that like to visit the club are usually wanting a chance to become a member.

Use Newspaper Ads with Caution

If you must resort to a newspaper ad, do it with caution. Take the time to write a good ad that will attract someone with like interests. A longer ad will cost more but it is better to let the reader know what you want. Here is an ad I saw when I was writing this book. The ad not only got the club a good member but there are four others on the waiting list for future membership openings.

> **Deer hunt club** membership available, $575 annually. 3500 acres on Sipsey River in Green Co. Only stalk hunting, 8-points or better, workday attendance a must. First year probation. Call Larry, 345-6789.

This ad told that it was a deer hunting club, that they only stalk hunted, that they only wanted those interested in quality deer management, that you must be interested in working on the property, and that you would be under the other members' watchful eye the first year. It told where the lease was located, how much the membership fee is, and the size of the lease. The reader knew a lot when he called the president and the president knew something of the prospective member's interest. A good ad will help with the screening from the beginning.

Other Sources of New Members

I have known clubs to get new members from clubs that adjoin their property or are located nearby. The new members didn't abandon one club for another but bought a membership so that they would have more property to hunt. Some clubs recruit new members from the area surrounding the hunt club property. If the adjoining landowners like your group, they may want to join. Conservation officers are often a good source of finding prospective members. Other organizations you or other members belong to may be a good source. I know of a club in Texas that got most of its startup members from a notice placed on a bulletin board at a sporting clays club. I know of another club that has filled its membership needs from two churches.

Regardless of how you find prospective members, take your time to get to know them and them to get to know your group. It's a long-term relationship and you want it to be good for everyone.

Special events, workdays, and hunts are good times to attract new members.

HANDLING POACHERS AND TRESPASSERS

Game law violators should not be handled by club members, but should be reported to professional wildlife officers.

I f your club owns or leases hunting property, it's a safe bet that sooner or later you are going to have to face the problems of poaching, trespassing, or a member game law violation. I know of few clubs who escape the situation. In fact, the better job you do of managing your land for quality deer the higher the risk you run of having poacher or trespasser problems. People who are prone to be wildlife criminals want to go where the best game animals are found.

Don't Invite Trouble

There are several things you can do to reduce the potential of problems of this type. First, be sure you have a well-marked boundary and check it regularly to make sure that people know when they cross over into your club's property. Have sturdy gates leading onto your property from public roads. Place posted signs along rivers or public roads that run through your club's property. Poorly marked property invites problems.

Maintain a good relationship with the local residents. The local crossroads store owner, rural mail carrier, neighbors, adjoining clubs, and your land-owner should become friends of the club. These people influence many of the local residents and they can help stop problems before they become problems. Make an enemy out of the local general store owner and he can encourage others to hunt on your property. He most likely knows when you are there and when you aren't. The same goes for any locals. Be a good neighbor and you will be rewarded.

In addition, it is a good idea to purchase supplies locally and patronize local businesses when you can as it builds a good relationship with the local peo-ple. Locate your club's skinning shed, meat pole, etc., out of view of public roads. Encourage club members to be most cautious about boasting about big deer seen or taken on the club. The same for gobblers. Hearing that the club is seeing or taking a lot of 140-plus B&C point bucks or gobblers with 10-inch beards can invite poachers.

Never locate food plots, camps, stands, or blinds within sight of public roads. The old saying "out of sight, out of mind" has a lot of truth in it.

Be Friends with the Local Law Enforcement

Nothing deters wildlife criminals, or a club member who is thinking about violating a game law, more than knowing that the sheriff, conservation officers, forest rangers, or highway patrolmen are frequent visitors of a hunting club. Find out who the local law enforcement officials are and invite them to stop by

Hunting club members and their vehicles should be easy to identify. This hunting club requires all member-vehicles to display this decal.

the club for coffee or lunch when they are patrolling in the area. Invite them to be a guest for a hunt and to attend cookouts.

These officers can be some of the best friends you can have, especially if your property is in a remote location. Ask them to check on the base camp or clubhouse during the off-season.

Have Club Members Well Identified

The larger the club the more you need to be able to identify each member and his vehicle. Regardless of club size, each club member should have a membership card on him at all times when on the club property. This allows law enforcement officers, the landowner, and unfamiliar club members to verify that he is

a member. Many members have a club patch sewn on a hat or hunting coat so that they can be identified as a club member at a distance.

All vehicles used on the club property should have a decal, bumper sticker, or cardboard pass on the dashboard so that it is obvious that the vehicle belongs to a club member. Many clubs that use ATVs, boats, or other type of vehicles require that some form of ID be attached to the vehicle. Some clubs require that stands or blinds have a club ID so that a poacher's blind can be identified easily.

Handling Poachers and Trespassers

Poachers, trespassers, and general wildlife criminals not only spoil the hunt for honest hunters but also can pose a physical threat when confronted or seen. During my years in wildlife law enforcement, I have seen these people threaten bodily harm, both out of disregard for their fellow man as well as fear. One can be as deadly as the other.

All hunting clubs should have a conservation officer and deputy sheriff come to a club meeting and give a program as to how to handle poachers and trespassers. The laws vary from state to state and don't assume you know it. The law enforcement agency that handles trespassers and poachers varies by county and the club should be briefed as to whom to call in the county in which the hunting property is located. In my home state, it is a common misbelief among hunting club members that you can legally shoot trespassers. It's not true and if you did, your life would change forever.

Making friends with the law enforcement officials in the county in which your club property is located assures your club of quick help when a problem occurs.

Law enforcement officers advise club members to avoid heated confrontations with poachers or trespassers. Give them space. Get the most accurate description of the person and/or vehicle that you can. Stay with the facts. Call the local sheriff's office or conservation officer as per the instructions given to you at the club meeting. Don't take the law into your own hands. Let

the law enforcement professionals do their job and you continue
being a hunter.

The club should have a policy to
prosecute any game law violators to
the fullest extent of the law. Trespass
law should be exercised as well.

Member Game Law Violators

This is perhaps the easiest part of
this book to understand. All hunting
clubs should have as a policy, and
stated in the bylaws and rules, that
any member violating a game law
will be turned in to law enforcement
officials as quickly as possible. Those
willfully violating game laws will
be terminated from the club membership. Accidents, such as shooting through a deer and killing two,
should be considered by the board
and if satisfied it was an accident, the
member should remain a member.

Hunting clubs cannot be successful
if they turn a deaf ear toward game
law violations. Those clubs who play
fair and report violations quickly
gain a good reputation with all concerned and the wildlife management
program benefits.

Proper posting of hunting club
property will help deter poaching
and trespass.

COMMUNICATION
BASICS

Good communications are a must and the more members a club has the more important communications become.

sk any experienced officer of a successful hunting club what is the one thing that holds the club together and he will tell you it is staying in touch with the members and letting them know what is going on. Back when I was working on a daily basis with a couple of hundred deer hunting clubs, which leased land from the company I worked for, I noticed how effective some clubs were at getting information out and how ineffective others were. The well-run clubs kept their members informed and up-to-date as to what was going on. The clubs that always had problems, and usually fell apart, were loosely run and the members didn't know what was going on. Good communications vital, especially in clubs with a large membership.

Officers Should Have Communications Skills

Since good communications start at the top, the hunting club president and the club secretary should be aware that there is a lot of information that the members need on a timely basis. When electing club officers, the members should look for officers that realize that communicating with the membership is vital to having a smooth running club. Information as basic as announcing club meetings and workdays well in advance to information as unexpected as the lessor planning a prescribed burn the opening day of spring turkey season is required to reach the members. Since some members may not live near other members and others may miss club meetings, it is necessary to have some means of informing members of club information in a timely manner.

Communication with hunting club members— by phone, e-mail, or newsletter— is the cement that holds the club together. This is especially true during the off-season.

Phone Network

Many small hunting clubs depend upon a telephone network to get the word out about upcoming meetings, special events, workdays, and membership news. It usually works like this—the president or other officer calls one member and tells him that the club will have a work weekend to plant food plots the third weekend of next month. Everyone should meet at the lease clubhouse on Saturday at 8:00 a.m. That member is required to call one or two assigned members to pass along the information. Upon receiving this information each of the members will call their assigned contacts.

This works well when the club is just six or eight members who are close friends; however, in larger clubs where lots of calls need to be made in a short period of time, the system can break down. Some of the members may be out of town and the chain of calls is broken. I have heard of club calling networks where the message was misinterpreted and the wrong or incorrect information was sent to several members.

Web Sites

In today's computer world, a growing number of hunting clubs, especially those with a webmaster in their membership, are developing a Web site for the club. The club member can log on and get up-to-the-minute information on the club. As I was working on this book I searched the Web and was surprised to see the number of hunting club Web sites out there. Many were interesting to visit and valuable information was available for the members. In addition, these might be a valuable recruiting tool for new membership.

The hunting club Web site would be a good consideration for clubs with large memberships, budgets that can afford the development cost and monthly fees, membership of computer owners, and a webmaster as a member who can keep the site current.

E-Mail

The fastest growing communications method used by hunting clubs is the use of e-mail. The president and/or secretary have a list of members' e-mail addresses and when a message needs to get out to the membership, it is simply typed and sent. It is fast and requires little work.

For e-mail to be effective, each member of the club needs to have Internet access and check his e-mail on a regular basis. One of the complaints I have heard from clubs that use e-mail is that the club's e-mails are excessive and go beyond being informative. Keeping the club's e-mails to pertinent club business and notices can keep this potential problem from happening.

Newsletter

Most of the clubs I have worked with or been a member of use a newsletter to keep members apprised of club activities. Some clubs use a desktop publishing software program to produce a nice newsletter, complete with photos. Others send a simple letter stating the information that needs to be conveyed. Both work if they are sent on a timely basis and are well written.

The desktop published newsletter is good for the club that has a budget that can stand the additional cost and a member that has the skills and time to do all the work. Lacking any of these resources, a letter can do a good job of keeping members up-to-date on the club's activities.

Remember Communication Basics

Regardless of the means of informing members of the club's activities, some basics need to be kept in mind:

▶ Keep the message(s) short, factual, and give complete details

▶ State the most important information first.

▶ Notify the members of meeting dates, dues due date, special events, and workdays as early as possible. Give them lots of planning time.

▶ Announce new members and tell a little about them.

▶ Inform members of off-season activities, i.e., fishing, shooting range for all-year leases. Make the lease valuable to the members to keep members in club.

▶ Make sure the lessor gets the information. An informed lessor is a happy lessor.

▶ Update members as to game law changes that affect the club property.

▶ Keep the club phone, e-mail, or mailing address list up-to-date.

SPECIAL EVENTS

Considering which hunting club to join was a difficult decision for Ron Taylor. He had lived in Dallas, Texas, all his life and knew many hunters who belonged to hunting clubs. Many of his friends had invited him to join their clubs and now that Ron could afford to join, he had several clubs to consider. Each club had a deer lease on a ranch within driving distance of Dallas. All the clubs were involved in the deer management on their lease and taking good bucks annually. They all sounded good and Ron couldn't decide which club to join.

One morning Ron was having breakfast with a fellow hunter who worked for the same company he did. During breakfast, the co-worker told him about kids weekend his club sponsored on their lease. Then he told Ron how on the weekend before deer season opened, the club had a sight-in day at the lease shooting range where the members helped one another sight-in their deer rifles. Finally, he told Ron that the club had an annual family cookout at the lease.

Being a family man and father of two grammar school age children, Ron now knew which hunting club he wanted to join. The benefit of special events made the difference.

One of the most valuable special events a hunting club can have is a youth hunt or a youth weekend on the club property.

It goes without saying that the main reason any of us join a hunting club is to have a good place to hunt where you know those in the woods with you. However, the more value you can get out of the club the more fun being a member. Special events help bring the members of the club closer together. Special events give other family members a look at the club and its property and make the club investment a little more meaningful to the whole family. Special events help recruit new members and help hold old members.

While not every club wants or needs special events, most find that some special events are valuable. Here are some, used by hunting clubs, to consider.

Annual Dinner
Get the spouses involved. Hold an annual dinner for the members and spouses. They have heard about all these members; let them see for themselves what characters they are. Some clubs do the annual dinner as a cookout and invite the entire family. Others do the covered-dish dinner and yet still, others have a catered meal.

Have a program after dinner. Give awards, or gag awards, to the members, with a story about each. A good conservation speaker makes a good program. Several larger clubs I know have a dance following the dinner. The point is it gives the spouses a chance to get to know more about the club and its members.

Wildlife Management Seminars
Most members of hunting clubs want to know more about the wildlife management on their club's property and would like to get involved. Often clubs have difficulty getting all members to see the advantages of shooting doe deer. Regardless of the reason, getting wildlife managers to conduct seminars is easy, inexpensive, and helps teach the members about the management of the wildlife they are hunting.

Wildlife programs such as hunter education, quality deer management, aging deer, how to have great food plots, and what to do when you have poachers

Cookouts and dinners that include family members permit hunting club members to share part of the benefit of their hunting club membership

make good topics. The local conservation officers, state game and fish agency wildlife biologists and others can supply a good program and they are there for the asking.

Sight-In Day

One of the most popular events at many clubs is an annual sight-in day at the club property or a nearby shooting range. It is amazing how many hunters do not know how to properly sight-in their firearms. Have several stations set up with experienced shooters manning each station. One station may be to clean the scope, another to bore sight rifles, another to actually shoot and adjust the riflescope at 100 yards, and a final station to clean the firearm.

Most clubs make this a one-day event complete with a cookout. It is a good service for the members. Many do not have a place to go to sight-in their firearms and this is a fun way to do it and get to know other members as well.

Above: Prior to hunting season, having a shooting range on the hunting club property gives the opportunity for all club members to sight-in their firearms.

Left: A youngster's opportunity to take his first deer on a parent's hunting club is a memory that will stay with him a lifetime.

Kids Day on the Lease

A few clubs I know have a popular event they call kids field day. It is a day that kids spend on the lease with some of the club members and state game and fish agency personnel teaching them about wildlife. Simple, short courses on wildlife tracks, identifying buck signs, identifying wild turkey signs, identifying trees, finding wildlife dens, etc., excite kids and they learn more about the hunting club. Who knows we may even get some future hunters out of each course.

Hunting clubs offer an
introduction to hunting for
the next generation.

Mock Trials

One of the most fun events I have ever attended is a mock trial held each year by three hunting clubs in central Alabama. The trial is planned for and look forward to for months each year. It is held at the end of deer season and anyone may be brought up on charges. Offenses such as loud snoring, missed shots, getting stuck, being late to the stand, etc., can get a member brought before the court.

The evening event begins with a big meal. Next, the appointed bailiff calls for order. The appointed judge then takes the bench. It is an honor to be selected as the judge as he is the only one immune from charges of wrongdoing. The judge appoints a prosecutor, a defense attorney, a small jury, and an executioner. The executioner cuts shirttails of those found guilty, that being most everyone.

The trial should be filmed, as it is the funniest two hours I have ever seen in a hunting camp. It has been a tradition with the group for more than two decades.

Cookout at Camp

A cookout at the hunting camp is a popular special event at many clubs. Family members, the landowner, conservation officers, and others who befriend the club are usually guests with the members doing the cooking. It is a good way to say thank you for past favors done, a great way for the member's family to see the club, and everyone gets to know one another better.

Have Special Events Well Organized

Special events are a good way to get all members in a hunting club involved with the club. The president should appoint committees to plan and organize each special event. The event should be promoted well in advance.

WHEN A MEMBER IS MISSING

A lot of hunters are taking survival courses and learning to "make do" in the event they should ever become lost or stranded, but very few know the proper steps to take if another member of their hunting club is suddenly missing.

A friend of mine was hunting deer with a group in a large swamp in the panhandle of Florida, when one night a hunter failed to show up for supper. No one knew where he had hunted that day, so two of the group took flashlights and went into the swamp in different directions. Three other members of the group got into their trucks and started driving up and down logging roads blowing their horns.

Around 2 a.m., someone went into town and got the local rescue squad, and around sunrise, they found the lost hunter.

When a hunting club member is missing, a predetermined course of action should be followed.

He had a complaint. Every time he had started toward the sound of a truck horn, it would move. He had spent the night unafraid, but he was worn out from chasing the ever-moving horns. As the hunters sat around camp eating breakfast and reliving the long night, someone suddenly realized that one of the two searchers who had gone into the swamp the night before with flashlights had not returned. Another search was under way. By late afternoon, the second man had been found in a state of total panic. Rather than hunt, the hunters spent the next two days in camp resting up for the trip home.

Those hunters had never considered that such a thing could happen to them, and when it did, they were unprepared. They acted out of panic, endangering the lost hunter as well as themselves.

Before you go into any back country area, recognize that it is one of the easiest places in which to get lost or stranded. Point out that fact to the other members of your group, and set up a system for keeping track of one another.

I occasionally hunt with a group of experienced deer hunters who camp and hunt on a lease made up mostly of swampy terrain. This club has a map of the property posted on a board, and each hunter, before leaving camp, must mark where he will hunt and when he plans to return. If the hunter changes locations, he must return to camp and change the map. This well-run camp has never had anyone lost for longer than an hour. A bonus of this system is that it keeps one hunter from accidentally spoiling the hunting of another.

It's a good idea for every outdoorsman to carry a police whistle. It makes locating him much faster. The sound of a whistle carries a long way.

When you work out a search plan with your group, stress how important it is for the lost person to stay put until contact is made. Have a prearranged set of signals. Don't do as the Florida group did and blow horns as you drive around. If you have a vehicle nearby, blow the horn, but keep the vehicle in one place.

If you or any of your companions have medical problems, see to it that the matter is common knowledge. If a member of your group has a heart problem, fainting spells, or the like, make sure that he has a "buddy" to accompany him. There is nothing more discouraging for searchers than to go into a camp that has lost a hunter or fisherman and hear that he is alone and has a medical problem. Too often, the story has a sad ending, which a little forethought could have prevented.

The most crucial time during a missing buddy situation is when you first realize that he is late coming into camp and you get no answers to your signals. Don't panic. Follow these simple guidelines.

The first rule is to stay calm and use your head, as the next few minutes may be the most important. In most cases, lost or stranded situations are merely a sobering two- to three-hour adventure. So, when a member of your group is suddenly missing, don't go to pieces. Overcome fear and THINK.

Well-organized hunting clubs usually have a property map upon which members and guests check the area in which they will be hunting. In the event of a missing hunter, this gives search and rescue personnel a starting point.

At the point the missing person was last seen or near the area he was going to, try blowing an automobile horn or police whistle. Either of these signals is an indication to the missing person that someone has missed him, and if he is

nearby, he can walk to the sound. For this reason, it is crucial that the signaling be done from one spot. This is an important part of the early search, as people who have been rescued often say that, while they were lost or stranded, they figured that no one would bother to look for them.

Serious search and rescue efforts should be turned over to professionals as early as possible.

When blowing a horn or whistle, blow it in bursts of three so that it is obvious to the missing person that someone is signaling him and it is not some unrelated noise. Pause between bursts and listen carefully for a reply. If the missing person has a whistle, you may hear a response immediately.

The last person to see the missing person should mark the spot where the person was last seen. Use a bright piece of cloth such as a handkerchief, bright orange cap, or hunting coat. It is extremely important that trained searchers be able to return to this spot to plan and begin their search. Too often, when searchers are called in to set up a search, valuable time is lost because no one can take them to the point the missing person was last seen. Highly skilled search and rescue workers can determine where the lost person is most likely to be, known as the "area of probability," if they can be taken quickly to the point last seen and given the approximate time the person was first missed.

As soon as you miss a member of your group and it is determined that he is in trouble, leave one or more persons at the spot last seen, or near the area in which it is suspected that the missing person is in, to blow a signal horn or whistle. Another person should seek out a forest ranger, conservation officer, or sheriff's department official as soon as possible to get trained search and rescue people on the scene.

Be able to give the searchers a great deal of information about the missing person. **Here is what most "search bosses" would like to know about a missing person:**

 ▸ Name and address of the missing person(s).

 ▸ Description.

 ▸ Purpose for being in the back country. Is he a hiker, hunter, etc?

 ▸ Age.

 ▸ Equipment he is carrying. Is he a hunter who has a daypack filled with equipment, or is he a hunter who has little more than the clothes he is wearing?

 ▸ Exact place last seen. His starting point is an important piece of data, because all search operations center around this point during the early phases of the search.

- Names, addresses, and phone numbers of all the people who were in the immediate area.

- Circumstances of the disappearance. Exactly when and where was the person discovered missing? Was he en route to somewhere? If so, where?

- Exactly how long has he been overdue?

- Type of footwear he is wearing. If possible, this includes a description of the sole pattern, which is useful for tracking.

- Color of clothing and equipment. This is helpful during a search, because items of clothing and equipment searchers find can be vital clues.

- Brands of such items as cigarettes, candy, and gum he has with him.

- Signal capabilities. Did he carry a whistle, flashlight, firearm, or any other method of signaling?

- Experienced in the outdoors? Has he had survival training? Has he been lost in the past?

- Physical condition. At the time he was lost, was he fatigued, depressed, cold, hungry, or ill? What medical problems, if any, does he have?

- Personality traits of the subject. Is he smart, realistic, confident, aggressive, moody, optimistic, or pessimistic?

- Does he have a good, positive mental attitude or is he immature, unsure, negative, shy, or depressed?

The answers to these questions can help greatly in finding a lost person.

These guidelines should be taught to all members of a group before a hunt into the back country begins. Most outdoor trips are taken with little or no preparation for a member to become lost or stranded.

Every lost person situation differs to some degree from others, but usually these basic rules will assure a speedy and orderly rescue. If the lost or stranded person is properly prepared, the whole event will be over quickly.

All club members should be trained in basic survival techniques in the unlikely event that they might have to spend an unplanned night in the woods.

By having a nutritious food crop growing in the plot all year, you will have healthier animals and hold them on the property easier.

PLANTING AND MANAGING FOOD PLOTS

There have been many books written on the planting and managing of food plots. I am the editor of a magazine that runs information on this subject on a monthly basis. We never run out of new information. This is to say that this chapter will not tell you everything you will want to know about the subject.

However, most hunting clubs which own or lease land eventually get involved in the improving of habitat for wildlife, and food plots are popular for this purpose. In fact, many clubs' members enjoy working with food plots as much as they do hunting. It can be a year-round activity and a thing of pride when someone takes a nice buck off a food plot he created and managed.

There are many different ways to manage food plots. What follows is a simple step-by-step process that most use in setting up and managing food plots. If your club gets land that already has plots, then you may stick to those. If your lease does not permit the creation of food plots, you may want to refer to chapter 25 on improving native plant species.

Many hunting clubs choose to hire a local farmer to plant their food plots. He has the equipment and experience to do the job quickly.

How Many Acres in Food Plots?

Most wildlife managers agree that land managed for deer and wild turkey needs to have at least one to three percent of the total acreage in openings. These openings need to be fairly well distributed across the acreage. With this in mind-set as your goal two percent of your hunt club in food plots. If you have a 1,000-acre lease, try to have 20 acres in food plots.

Size of Food Plot

I have seen clubs with food plots that only averaged 1/8 to 1/4 acre in size. These food plots were eaten up quickly and often little game was seen on them. On the other hand, I have seen some clubs that had food plots that were 20 acres or more in size. These were heavily used at night but only around the edges were many deer seen during daylight hours. Not good for the hunter.

Breaking the ground on a food plot can be done easily by a tractor pulling a set of disks.

During the years I managed Westervelt Hunting Lodge in Alabama, we tested food plots ranging in size from 1/4 acre to 15 acres. Keeping records of deer sighted and taken on these plots, we found that the food plots that were 2 acres in size were the most productive for deer harvest. They were large enough to produce a lot of food but small enough to escape from easily. They attracted a lot of does and consequently a lot of bucks.

Ever since then, I have used 2-acre food plots in various parts of the United States and have been pleased with the results.

Shape of Food Plots

The shape of food plots is often dictated by the opening you have to work with. If you are using an old road or gas line right of way, then you have little choice but to have long, narrow food plots. However, if your club should be so lucky as to have the food plots take any shape you wish, then you should strive to have 2-acre plots that are rectangular in shape.

Don't guess at the size of a food plot because the amount of lime, fertilizer, and seed you will use will be based on the actual size of the plot. Use a range finder or steel tape and take the time to accurately measure the size of the plot. Then record the size for future use.

Try to have plots without trees out in the opening. Trees make planting difficult, competing with the crop planted for water and sunlight. You will want plots that have sunlight on them at least 50 percent of the day.

Sites for Food Plots

When looking for potential sites for food plots consider existing openings. Log landings (decks), old forest roads, old homesites, abandoned fields, utility rights of way, and gas lines have all been used to make good food plots. Try to select those that have the most fertile soil. Remember that food plots located in bottomland generally make the best food plots due to the soil being moister. If you must create food plots in forest, use a bulldozer to clear the site and work to remove all stumps and roots.

Avoid sites where livestock can get into the food plots. Avoid placing plots near property boundaries or public roads, as you will be inviting trouble. Select sights where wildlife has escape cover adjacent to the plots. I once visited a hunting club that had located a number of good-looking food plots out in a two-year-old clear-cut. They couldn't understand why the deer only used the plots at night. It was obvious that deer had to cross a quarter mile of open country to reach the food plots. Some of the most productive food plots I have ever seen are those located adjacent to a swamp or thick creek bottom. Bucks felt safe in leaving the thick cover a few steps to feed on the lush planted crop.

Using an aerial photo or topo map of the property mark, each potential food plot site and make sure that they are not all in one end of the property. You want these wildlife food "platters" to be about evenly distributed across the property.

Food plot preparation and planning may be done with an ATV pulling one of the latest generation food plot preparation attachments.

Electrically powered seeders, available for ATVs, are ideal for fertilizing and seeding food plots.

Name Your Club's Food Plots

There is nothing I hate worse than to visit a hunting club to help them with their deer management program and discover that no one to knows what food plot is being discussed. If for no other reason, management should give each plot a name and record it on the club map. If an old mule barn had to be torn down to create the plot, name it Mule Barn Field. Then when you are calculating fertilizer or discussing a large buck seen there, when you say Mule Barn Field everyone thinks of the same plot. Besides, it is fun to come up with all the names and adds a sense of permanence to the property.

Some clubs assign a food plot to a member or team of members to be responsible for its management. It can become a fun competition and it gets all the members into the management of the club property.

Plan the Plot Management and Soil Test Each Food Plot

Once the food plots are selected and created, it is time to come up with a management plan for each plot. Here you should get a wildlife professional involved to help you plan the crops that should be planted. I would

encourage any club to have a spring planting program and a fall planting program. By having a nutritious food crop growing in the plot all year, you will have healthier animals and hold them on the property easier. Set up a record on each plot so that you can keep a record of soil test results, fertilizer history, recommended plant choices, planting dates and harvest records. Having a record on each plot allows the club and their wildlife professional a chance to see the plot history and aids in improving the plot's performance in the future.

To have a healthy wildlife food plot, take a soil test. The results of this test will tell you how to fertilize and lime the ground for proper balance of nutrients and optimum soil pH level. Time and money are saved when you apply only the fertilizer needed. Overfertilization may cause harm to plant materials and waste your hunting club money.

▶ Go to your local county agent's office (Cooperative Extension Service) and get a soil test kit. It will consist of soil sample bags, information sheets, and shipping box. Do-it-yourself soil test kits may be purchased from garden supply stores also.

- Get the tools you will need to take the samples—a clean bucket and a clean garden trowel, spade, or soil probe.

- Follow the information given in the soil test kit directions to select several sites to take samples.

- At each test site in the yard or field, scrape off any plant material from the soil surface. Push the trowel into the soil 3 to 4 inches deep.

- Discard the soil and cut an-inch slice from the back of the hole. Place the slice in the bucket. Do this at each test site.

- Thoroughly mix the slices and pour them into the sample bag.

- Mark the bag with the required information.

- Send the bag to the state-testing lab listed in the kit instructions. A small fee is usually charged.

- You will receive the test results with recommendations as to amounts and types of fertilizer and lime needed for your intended crop. Follow the recommendations to the letter. Wildlife knows the difference between a cheap hamburger and prim steak. The food plot planted following the recommendations of a current soil test is "prime steak."

Lime the Plot Early

According to Alabama Game and Fish Division biologists, liming food plots is an affordable way

---

Fertilizing and seeding the food plot can be done simply by using a hand-operated seeder.

to provide the elements necessary for optimum growth and nutrition of plants, which in turn benefits the animals that eat the plants.

Low soil acidity reduces the productivity of small-grain crops more than any other soil fertility condition. Soil pH is the measure of the concentration of hydrogen ions in the soil solution. The pH range of a soil solution indicates whether it is acid, neutral, or alkaline. A pH of 7 is neutral. The higher the H ion concentration, the more acid the soil.

What does all this have to do with wildlife food plots? Most forage crops (clover, sorghum, corn, millet, wheat and rye) do very well when properly fertilized and established on soil with a pH of 5.8 to 6.5. Proper liming will maintain soil pH within this range while supplying necessary plant nutrients such as calcium and magnesium.

Liming will ensure maximum use of fertilizers applied to the wildlife openings. To begin a liming program, ask your county Cooperative Extension Service office for soil sample boxes. To get proper lime and fertilizer recommendations, be sure to follow the recommended procedures for taking the samples.

Then mail the soil samples to the state soil-testing lab. For about $7 per sample, the soil will be tested. A recommendation for lime and fertilizer specifically tailored to your soil type and the forage species you plan to plant will be mailed to you.

The author prefers a short-toothed harrow pulled by an ATV for smoothing food plots and covering seeds.

After you receive your analysis, again contact your county Cooperative Extension Service office to get valuable information on the local cost of lime, as well as contacts for possible suppliers. Lime at least four months before you plant your wildlife crop. It takes time for agricultural lime to break down.

Remember, adding liming to your management program will help supply wildlife with the essential chemical elements for growth, energy, reproduction, and antler development.

Clear and Mow Plot before Breaking Ground

The first step toward having a good food plot is to walk the plot and look for anything that might cause problems when breaking the ground or planting. Look for rocks and roots. If you are breaking ground in the spring, look for shed antlers. I have had more than one expensive tractor tire ruined by a shed antler being run over.

After the plot has been examined, mow the plot to make the cutting up of weeds and old crop easier. This can be done with a pull-behind mower towed by a tractor or an ATV. I have used both with satisfaction; however, the tractor mower cuts the time down dramatically.

Break the Ground and Prepare a Good Seedbed

Breaking ground in food plots, liming and fertilizing, preparing a seedbed, planting, and covering seed require some farming equipment and know-how. Before your club decides to tackle the chore yourselves, consider hiring a local farmer who has the equipment and experience to do the job. Often, he will do it just as cheaply as your club can do it and in a fraction of the time, doing it right the first time.

In many cases, hunting clubs have property that is remote and not near a farmer. In other cases, clubs enjoy the weekends spent planting food plots and wouldn't consider letting anyone else have the fun of doing it. (The number of hunting club

No-Plow mix was sown on the right half of this field with only the ground being lightly scratched.

members enjoying the farming of food plots is growing.) If this is your club's case, then you will want to take each step of planting seriously.

Preparing the Seedbed

If you have a farmer as a member of your hunting club, then you may have access to a tractor, planting equipment, and know-how. A tractor can save you a lot of time when breaking the ground of a food plot and smoothing the seedbed. Since most food plots are small, I like to use a small tractor, 25–32 HP, as they work well in tight places yet have the muscle to break ground easily.

The ATV of today, 400cc and larger with four-wheel drive, can be used to break ground in well-established food plots. Attachments, such as the Woods-N-Water Plotmaster, are designed to do all the functions of food plot planting using an ATV. There is also a Plotmaster designed for tractors.

For breaking the ground, I like to use an offset disk or a tandem disk. Be sure to schedule the groundbreaking time when the soil is reasonably dry. Go over the plot several times breaking the soil to a depth of four inches or more. Break up clumps of soil and level the plot as much as you can. Two to three passes with a disk properly adjusted will usually result in a good job. Next, level the plot. I like to use a short-toothed harrow pulled behind my ATV for this purpose. The ATV allows me to get into the corners easier.

Properly done, food plots can become the pride and job of the hunting club with the benefit going to wildlife.

Fertilizing, Planting, and Covering Seed

With a well broken-up and leveled plot, I am assuming the plot has been properly limed several months previously, you are ready to plant the seed based on the seed producer's recommended rate and depth.

Some food plot planters like to use their seeders and mix fertilizer and seed and sow both at the same time. I prefer to distribute the fertilizer, at the recommended rate, with my seeder and then sow the seed. If you use a seeder to distribute fertilizer, be sure to wash the seeder well after fertilizing, as the residual will corrode the seeder in a short period.

For seeding the plot, you can use a hand seeder, an electrical seeder attached to an ATV, or a PTO powered tractor mounted seeder. For very small food plots the hand seeder will work well; however, for larger plots the ATV or tractor seeder saves time and gets more uniform seed coverage. I prefer the electrical seeder mounted on an ATV, as it gets into tight places easier than a tractor and can do the job quickly.

After sowing the seed, you will need to cover the seed as per the seed producer's recommendation. You can use one of several methods to cover seeds. A section of cyclone fencing pulled behind a tractor will do the job. A heavy timber pulled behind a tractor or an ATV will cover seed. I like to use my short-toothed harrow turned upside down so the smooth side is on the ground. It has enough weight to cover the seeds but not enough to cover them too deeply.

With the seed covered, all you have to do now is to hope for rain.

No-Till planting

In food plots where you have a permanent planting of perennial warm season grasses, you can plant a cool season annual crop to attract game by using the method called no-till planting. It requires a special no-till planter and some special skill in using it. I would suggest contacting the county agricultural agent in the county where your hunt club land is located to find someone to do your no-till planting.

To measure the amount of use a food plot is getting, you can erect an exclusion cage such as this one to see how much the deer are eating the food plot crop outside the cage.

Another no-till situation is where you may want to plant a small food plot in a remote location where you can't get farm equipment. Here you can scratch up the ground using an ATV with a small disk or you can manually scratch up the surface with a hand rake. Next, use a hand seeder and fertilize the site. Following this, seed the area with a seed mixture called Imperial No-Plow. Follow the seed producer's planting instructions.

There are several seeds that will germinate and grow when seeded on bare or scratched soil but the results depend upon how much rain you get just after you sow them (they can wash away), how much sunlight the site gets, and how many birds find the exposed seed. Don't expect the same results from this quick fix as a properly prepared seedbed.

Planting Guide for Deer

SPRING FOOD PLOT CROPS FOR DEER

ALL STATES

Species	Planting months (after danger of frost)	Planting rate/ac (broadcast)	Annual/Perennial
American Joint Vetch	May-June	15 lbs/ac	Annual
Buckwheat	May-June	40 lbs/ac	Annual
Cowpeas	June	2 bu/ac	Annual
Grain Sorghum	May	30 lbs/ac	Annual
Iron Clay Peas	May	50 lbs/ac	Annual
Kobe Lespedeza	March	30 lbs/ac	Annual
Lablab	May	45 lbs/ac	Annual
Soybean	May	60 lbs/ac	Annual

FALL FOOD PLOT CROPS FOR DEER

NORTHERN STATES

Species	Planting months	Planting rate/ac (broadcast)	Annual/Perennial
Alfalfa	Aug. & Sept.	20 lbs/ac	Perennial
Alsike Clover	Aug. & Sept.	12 lbs/ac	Perennial
Birdsfoot Trefoil	Aug. & Sept.	5 lbs/ac	Perennial
Ladino Clover	Aug. & Sept.	5 lbs/ac	Perennial
Red Clover	Aug. & Sept.	14 lbs/ac	Annual
Sweet Clover	Aug. & Sept.	14 lbs/ac	Biennial
Timothy	Aug. & Sept.	8 lbs/ac	Perennial
Turnips	Aug. & Sept.	4 lbs/ac	Annual
Wheat	Aug. & Sept.	100 lbs/ac	Annual

SOUTHERN STATES

Species	Planting months	Planting rate/ac (broadcast)	Annual/Perennial
Arrowleaf Clover	Sept. & Oct.	10 lbs/ac	Annual
Austrian Winter Peas	Sept.	30 lbs/ac	Annual
Crimson Clover	Sept. & Oct.	20 lbs/ac	Annual
Hairy Vetch	Sept. & Oct.	20 lbs/ac	Annual
Ladino Clover	Sept.	5 lbs/ac	Perennial
Turnips	Sept.	4 lbs/ac	Annual
Winter Wheat	Sept.	100 lbs/ac	Annual

Measuring the Results of a Food Plot

It's an old question: Is the glass half full or half empty? This can apply to food plots planted for deer. When you walk up to the plot, the crop height usually looks the same over most of the field. There is little indication of how much forage the crop has produced or how much has been eaten by deer.

One way to keep tabs on food plot utilization is to construct an exclusion barrier, sometimes called exclusion cage, on each plot. This prevents deer and other animals from eating on the small area within the barrier. You can see how much forage the field is producing and, by comparison, how much the deer are eating.

You can make a simple exclusion barrier from a piece of welded wire fence at least 5 feet tall and rolled to 3 feet in diameter. Be sure the mesh is small enough so deer can't stick their noses through the fence and eat inside.

Wire the roll shut, and place it in the middle of the food plot when the plot is planted. Then stake the fence to keep animals from knocking it over.

Be sure to remove the exclusion barrier or mark it with bright tape before mowing or breaking the plot. When growers build an exclusion barrier on a food plot, many who think their plots are getting little use are surprised at how much forage deer actually have eaten.

AN ARTIFICIAL SALT LICK

Early American hunters quickly learned that a natural salt lick was a good place to see deer and other wildlife. Natural salt licks have been favorite hunting grounds for centuries. Today, wildlife managers use man-made salt or mineral licks to attract wildlife. In many cases, mineral licks are a feeding supplement that provides deer with calcium, phosphorus, iron, and zinc. This can be important when bucks are growing antlers and young deer begin to feed on their own.

Before you go to the trouble to put salt or mineral licks on your property, be sure to ask your local conservation officer if you can legally install and hunt near them.

In some states, putting in licks is legal, but you cannot hunt near them. In other states, you can hunt around salt licks but not mineral licks.

> Today, wildlife managers use man-made salt or mineral licks to attract wildlife.

These before and after shots show the use deer make of a salt lick made around a stump.

Almost any stump can be converted into a salt lick.

How to Make the Lick

Most wildlife managers prefer to use granular salt or minerals rather than blocks. Blocks must melt and run into the soil before deer and other wildlife can use them. This takes a lot of rain and time. Granular salt or minerals dissolve and are utilized quickly.

Deer usually find salt or mineral licks regardless of their location, but many wildlife managers like to put a lick in the corner or along the edge of a good plot (in areas where it is legal to hunt near them).

While these licks are used year around the period of heaviest use is usually during summer and early fall—a plus if viewing wildlife during summer is important. Also, this is the time you want to have as many buck attractants as possible. Salt licks are a great place to set up a photo blind during the nonhunting season to observe and photograph deer and other wildlife.

Bring Deer to the Lick

One of the most natural looking salt licks is an old stump. Using posthole diggers, dig deep holes under the stump between the roots. Pack the holes with granular salt or minerals. Put some on top of the stump so that deer can find the lick faster. After two or three rains, deer usually find the salt source and return often to enjoy it. When I had hunting lodges I used salt around stumps in new food plots to encourage deer to dig up the stumps. It works over a period of time.

If a stump is not where you want a salt lick, you can create a lick by digging a hole 2 feet deep in the ground and 3 feet across. Pour in a sack of granular salt keeping a little to put on top. Cover the hole containing salt with dirt and put a little salt on top so the deer will find it quickly. Salt licks of this type work well in the corner of a food plot or near a patched of fertilized honeysuckle.

It takes a while for the salt to melt into the soil and for the deer to find it but when they do, they will dig the hole much deeper.

One bag of salt usually lasts six to eight months. Many wildlife managers sweeten up the stump only once a year. When deer start using a lick, they often dig a stump up in a year or two.

A QUICK-GROW OAK FOOD PLOT

W e often spend so much time working to have good food plots that we forget that we can have a permanent food plot just by planting fast-growing oaks in a grove. One oak that produces acorns in a short period of time is the sawtooth oak. Not only do these oaks produce acorns at an early age, they produce lots of acorns when they are properly cared for.

Where Did They Come From

The Sawtooth oak, which gets its name from the serrated edge of the leaf, was imported into the United States from Asia in the 1920s as an ornamental tree. A species of white oak, the sawtooth is a fast-growing tree that may reach 50 to 70 feet in height.

Sawtooth oaks may be planted for a fast-growing food supply that will last for many years.

Sawtooth oaks must be protected from beavers when planted near streams or lakes.

The tree is still new enough to the United States that the full extent of its range is not known. However, it is doing well throughout much of the eastern half of the country into southern New England, west through East Texas, and north to south-central Michigan.

The sawtooth oak doesn't do well in areas where winter temperatures frequently dip below 0°F for long periods.

Fast Producers

Hunting clubs that are interested in managing wild turkeys, deer, squirrels, and other mast-eating wildlife like the sawtooth oak's ability to produce acorns at an earlier age, often as early as the fifth to eighth year. Some researchers have reported well-managed trees bearing acorns as early as the fourth year.

Our research with sawtooth oaks at my Cross Creek Hollow farm has recorded initial acorn production between the fifth and eighth years. Trees planted out in the open that are fertilized and kept free of competitive plants are the first to bear acorns.

Whether these trees bear acorns in the fourth year of growth or the ninth, this is still much faster than the 20 to 30 years it takes other species of oak to produce their first mast crop.

An Abundance of Large Acorns

Sawtooth oak trees that are 20 to 25 years old reportedly have produced 1,000 to 1,300 pounds of acorns in one year. Considering that there are 50 to 80 acorns in a pound, that's a lot of fall and winter food for wildlife.

The average sawtooth acorn is 1 1/4 inches long. Because wild turkeys prefer smaller acorns, researchers in Kentucky developed a new variety of sawtooth oak, called the Gobbler. It produces 5/8- to 3/4-inch acorns and yields about 150 acorns per pound.

Planning for Success

The sawtooth oak, like any other high-yield plant, must be planted with care if it is to give satisfactory results. The seedling has a large carrot-like taproot that must be set out with the point straight down, not bent, into a "J" shape. The roots must be completely covered.

The sawtooth requires sunlight 75 percent of the day, so it does best when planted in open fields or large forest openings. At Cross Creek Hollow, we planted several seedlings in shady areas six years ago. Today, they are only one foot taller than when we set out the seedlings.

Setting out sawtooths near pine plantations as a source of food near cover for deer and wild turkeys is a good idea. However, sawtooths must be planted far enough away from the pines to prevent overshading.

During the first three to five years of growth, sawtooth seedlings cannot stand competition from grass, weeds, trees or other plants, so it is necessary to mechanically control vegetation around the seedlings. When setting seedlings out in a large field, space them so that a tractor with a mower or disk can be driven between the trees easily.

In an orchard-style planting, wildlife biologist Joel Martin with the Alabama Game & Fish Division recommends a 20- x 25-foot spacing. The heaviest use by wild turkeys and deer is reported where the "orchards" are about a half acre in size.

Proper fertilization can increase growth and mast production. In the absence of a soil test, an application of 13-13-13 fertilizer broadcast in a 6-foot circle around the trees usually works well.

Sawtooth oaks grow best in well-drained soils. Although they adapt to a variety of soils, seedlings grow poorly in a deep sand and in areas that retain water.

Sawtooth oak acorns are produced on sawtooth oak trees beginning at about age 8 years.

Beavers Also Love Them

It has been our experience at Cross Creek Hollow that beavers will travel quite a distance to cut down and carry away sawtooth oak trees that are in their fifth year of growth. If you are establishing sawtooths within a quarter-mile of a known beaver population, it is wise to protect the tree trunk.

In addition, deer can browse young trees to the point of killing of stunting them. It may be necessary to place heavy wire cages around young trees until the branches are out of browsing reach. I like to use 6-inch plastic drainpipe cut down the side to spread apart and slip over the young tree trunks. I have never had a beaver get to a tree that had this type of protection.

Where to Get Seedlings

A number of state forestry agencies offer sawtooth oaks to landowners. A good source for sawtooth oaks and the new Gobbler sawtooth is Project HELP (Habitat Enhancement Land Program).

This program, which is sponsored by the National Wild Turkey Federation, makes seed and seedlings that are of value to wildlife available at competitive prices.

Write to Project HELP, Dept. RS, National Wild Turkey Federation, Box 530, Edgefield, SC 29824; or phone 1-800-843-6983.

I like to find a natural food source that animals like and improve its quality. This gives you the ability to have food plots in remote areas and keep the location private.

NATURAL SOURCE FOOD PLOTS

My favorite type of food plot is not one where you plant an acre or more of a crop wildlife likes to eat. I like to find a natural food source that animals like and improve its quality. This gives you the ability to have food plots in remote areas and keep the location private. A growing number of hunting clubs are doubling the number of food plots they have on their leases by fertilizing honeysuckle and smilax (greenbrier) patches, persimmon trees, oak trees, and blackberry patches, all producing food favored by deer and other species of wildlife. Some clubs use only this type of food plots.

The Honeysuckle Food Plot

Japanese honeysuckle, a woody evergreen vine, is a favorite food of deer. As its name implies, the plant was introduced into the United States from Asia. It grows well in shade and much better in direct sunlight.

Known for its hardiness, it tolerates drought and cold weather, and it is difficult to extricate in areas where it is not desired. It produces an abundance of leaves, stems, and seed that are a preferred food source for deer, as well as rabbits, quail, and wild turkey.

Acorn production can be increased on oak trees that are fertilized annually.

Fruit-bearing persimmon trees respond well to fertilization and provide a valuable food source for deer and other wildlife...

A study conducted by the Alabama Agricultural Experiment Station found that fertilizing a stand of honeysuckle can almost double its forage production. This also increases the plant's palatability and increases the crude protein content 11 to 17 percent.

The study showed that a fertilized honeysuckle patch averaged more than 2,480 pounds of forage. Honeysuckle is available to deer year round.

Managing a Stand

Here is how to manage the honeysuckle stands on your hunting club or farm:

- If possible, soil test each plot to determine the lime and fertilizer needs of the plants.

- In the absence of a soil test, apply 100 pounds of ammonium nitrate (34-0-0) and 300 pounds of 13-13-13 fertilizer per acre.

- Fertilize in early spring before green-up.

- Every 60 days after the first application, top-dress the stand with 100 pounds per acre of 34-0-0. Discontinue during periods of drought to avoid damaging the stand. Applying 34-0-0 just before a rain is always best. Discontinue in September.

- Fertilized honeysuckle will quickly climb trees out of reach of deer. To solve this problem, cut partly through the tree about 4 feet from the ground, then bend the top of the tree or shrub toward the ground to form a trellis. The vines can then grow within reach.

Other woods plants such as smilax and blackberry can be managed in the same way as honeysuckle and be included in your hunting club's wildlife management plan.

Before introducing any other new plants to your management plan, be sure to check with your county agent to make sure it is not considered to be an aggressive or undesirable plant for your area.

Fertilizing Mast-Producing Trees

Trees that produce mast such as oak, persimmon, and beech can be selected to fertilize and the mast crop can be both increased and made more attractive to deer. This same technique can be used on fruit trees, such as apple trees, found at old homesites.

Oaks should be selected with the help of a forester, as you will be looking for trees that are mature, usually over 25 years of age. You will want to select only oak trees that have a crown that is above the surrounding forest canopy and that gets a lot of sunlight.

I look for white oak trees that are known acorn producers to fertilize.

I look for white oak trees that are known acorn producers to fertilize. If there is competition from poor-quality trees around them, I cut those down to allow as much light to reach the acorn producer as possible. Persimmon trees must be selected based on observation of mast crops because if you select the wrong tree, no amount of management will produce fruit. Only the female tree is a fruit producer and this is determined by selecting trees that are known to have fruit.

Fertilizing mast-producing trees should be done in early spring. The rate is two pounds of 13-13-13 fertilizer per 1,000 square feet of crown. An oak with a crown measuring 60 by 70 feet (4,200 square feet) would require 8 pounds of fertilizer. A persimmon with a crown measuring 10 by 10 feet would need only 2 pounds of fertilizer.

Fertilizer should be spread using a hand seeder and walking around the tree in a circle in line with the outer edge of the crown, called drip line. Many people have a tendency to overfertilize trees, so resist the old adage if a little bit does a little bit of good, a lot will do a lot of good.

Also, remember that mast-producing trees will not produce mast every year regardless of how much tender loving care you give them. A lot of factors are at play, not the least of which is weather.

When fertilizing any mast-producing tree, it is best to use a hand seeder and to walk around the tree following the drip line.

It's a good idea to include
a provision in the club rules
that requires members to keep
accurate harvest records.

GATHERING DEER HARVEST DATA

I f you claim to manage your hunting club property for deer but don't keep harvest records, your claim is unjustified. Any wildlife professional requires a detailed deer-harvest record for the past few years (the more years the better) before making long-term management recommendations for your property.

Accurate records allow the wildlife manager to evaluate such characteristics as body condition, age structure, antler quality, and reproductive performance of the deer population on a tract of land. This information, together with a habitat condition study, allows the manager and the landowner to make informed decisions about harvest and habitat management.

Gathering harvest data is usually easy on property being hunted by a family. Getting all members of the hunting club to record the information can be difficult. It's a good idea to include a provision in the club rules that requires members to keep accurate harvest records.

Record-keeping for white-tailed deer involves removing the lower jawbone to determine the age of the animal. When properly done, this does not destroy the cape for taxidermy use.

The club should keep on hand at the deer cleaning station a deer-harvest record sheet or book and a supply of jawbone tags. Data from a harvested deer are written on a tag, which is then attached to the jawbone by a wire. Information from all tags is transferred to the deer-harvest record.

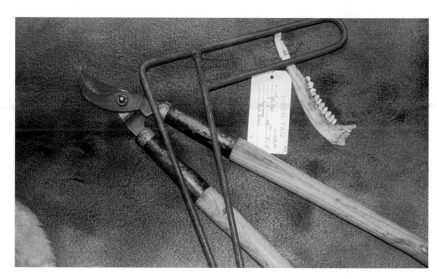

Tools for removing jawbones from deer are a jawbone extractor, lopping shears, and a jawbone tag.

You'll need a few items to gather deer harvest data, beginning with a scale for accurate weights. Most managers prefer live weights. If it is not practical to bring deer in for weighing before field dressing, then field-dressed weight is indicated on the forms.

Also, make sure you have lopping shears and a jawbone extractor for pulling the deer's lower jawbone to examine premolar and molar teeth—this is how deer are aged. A flexible steel or cloth tape is needed for measuring the antlers of the bucks taken.

You should also have a storage facility to keep jawbones safe from dogs, coyotes, opossums, and other critters. A freezer is best, but a well-ventilated wooden box with a secure lid is a good alternative. Many clubs keep deer jaws in a fish basket hung so that animals cannot get to it. In the basket, the jawbones dry quickly and do not stink as bad if they are hung outside.

Designate a check station where your equipment can be kept out of the weather and where a hoist is available for weighing deer.

Extracting a Deer Jawbone for Aging

The simplest and most accurate method wildlife professionals use for aging deer is extracting a lower jawbone and examining the tooth wear. When properly executed, this process doesn't harm the cape for mounting.

Here is how to extract a jawbone:

▶ Use a jawbone extractor, available from wildlife management tool suppliers listed in the Appendix of this book, to pry open the deer's mouth. Rigor mortis stiffens the jaw muscles quickly. Then, insert the smaller, rounded end of the extractor between the jawbone and cheek to break loose membrane and muscle.

Hold the deer's mouth wide open using the extractor. Insert the lopping shears with the blunt edge on the cheek side. Tilt the handle of the lopping shears toward the top of the head, and cut the jawbone.

Insert the smaller end of the jawbone extractor over the jawbone where the cut was made. With the deer's head held down firmly, give the extractor a quick tug. It should slide along the jawbone and break loose all muscles, freeing the jawbone. That side of the jawbone will separate from the opposite side near or in the middle of the front teeth. Only the premolars and molars are used in aging; the front teeth have no value for this purpose.

All jawbones pulled for aging should be tagged with pertinent information on the deer from which the jaw came.

Clean the jawbone and remove all tissue. Attach a tag for recording the data.

What You Should Record

Here is a list of information to record on each deer:

Deer number. Assign consecutive numbers to harvested deer. Write the number of extracted jawbones with an indelible pen.

State tag number. If the state requires a deer tag, record it.

Date of harvest.

Sex of harvest.

Antler measurements. Take inside-spread width, number of points, right and left beam lengths, and right and left beam circumference.

Weight of the deer. Use live or field-dressed weight.

Age. If the wildlife manager of the property is not present when you fill out the tag, leave it blank until he can examine the deer jawbone.

Doe lactation. If a doe is harvested, cut into the udder to see if milk is present.

Name of hunter.

What Do the Records Tell?

Whether you have a small club where only three deer are harvested or a large tract of land where 30 are taken, the information is valuable to the deer manager responsible for the property.

Knowing the age of harvested deer allows wildlife managers to classify and evaluate them by age. Body weights tell about the condition of the deer and the habitat. Antler measurements tell about the overall condition of male animals.

For example, on most lands not in a trophy buck management program, the 1 2/3-year-old buck is an indicator of the condition of the entire herd. That is because the majority of bucks harvested are in this age class.

Good weights (120 pounds in most areas) and a high percentage of fork-antlered, 1 1/2-year-old bucks indicate good overall herd health. Low weights and a large number of spikes in this age class suggest the herd may be exceeding the carrying capacity of the habitat.

Doe lactation data is quite valuable. If a doe is lactating when harvested, she has successfully reared a fawn. However, if several 3 1/2-year-old does are not lactating, the herd has a problem.

Within a herd that is in good condition, 20 to 30 percent of yearling does will be lactating. This means a high percentage of fawns are breeding earlier than normal, indicating a well-nourished herd.

A successful deer hunter admires the outcome of
effective hunt club game management. The same
techniques that yield top-quality bucks will benefit
a wide variety of game animals.

Appendix A   Sample Hunt Club Bylaws

Article I
The name of this organization shall be:

_____

Article II
PURPOSE

1. To abide by all requirements of the landowner;

2. To abide by all federal and state game laws and seasons;

3. To establish, foster, and promote an organization that provides an equitable, enjoyable, and harmonious outdoor environment for all club members; and

4. To participate in and promote a quality deer management program and management of all other wildlife species.

Article III
GOVERNING BODY

1. Directors

A. The affairs and business of this club shall be conducted by the board of directors. The board of directors will consist of at least five (5) directors who will each serve for a period of year(s), or until such time as his successor in office has been duly elected and qualified to succeed him.

B. The officers of the club (President, Vice President, Secretary and Treasurer) shall be elected annually.

C. The board of directors shall be elected by majority vote of the membership present at a called meeting. If an elected board member is unable to complete his term, the club shall elect another director to complete the rest of the term.

D. The board of directors is authorized to act on behalf of the club in all matters of club business, including (but not limited to) the following:

1) Propose rules and rule changes for the club. Any rule or rule change must be approved by 2/3 (67%) vote of club membership present at a called meeting.

2) Discipline any member, including dropping that member from the club.

3) Make any decision/restriction necessary regarding the deer management program on the club.

4) Assign committees, call workdays, etc., so that all members participate in the working needs of the club.

5) Set annual dues and assessments as required for lease payment and annual operation of the club.

E. The duties of the officers shall be as follows:

1) President – preside over all board and club meetings and functions.

2) Vice President – preside over all board and club meetings and functions in the absence of the President. Assume the position of the President should the elected President be unable to complete his term.

3) Secretary – record minutes for all board and club meetings. Handle all correspondence between club and landowner.

4) Treasurer – handle all income, payments and expenditures on behalf of the club.

Article IV
MEMBERSHIP

1. Membership of Club is limited to a maximum of 25 members.

2. A member may participate and/or vote in any called meeting by being present at the meeting or by submitting a written and signed proxy before the meeting. A quorum for purposes of voting at a called meeting will be set at 51% of the total membership or represented by proxy.

3. A member is responsible for his guest(s) and their actions.

4. All members and their guests must register at the camp, the purpose of their visit to the club, and all game harvested on club property in the log book at camp. All required deer data must be recorded for all deer harvested on the club.

5. The club reserves the right to expel, by a majority vote of 2/3 (67%) of the members present at a called meeting, any member for good cause or who does not conform to the stated purpose of the club. All club members must be notified in writing at least 10 days prior to a meeting called for this purpose. Any member expelled by the club forfeits all dues and is not due any compensation from the club.

6. A prospective membership list will be maintained by the board of directors for the purpose of evaluating prospective new members and filling vacancies with the club. All prospective new members must complete an Application for Membership.

7. A prospective new member must be approved by a majority vote of 2/3 (67%) of the membership present at a called meeting. If approved, a prospective new member will be admitted on a probationary basis for a period of one (1) year. Upon completion of the probationary year, he will be evaluated to full membership status or be dismissed from the club.

Article V
GUESTS

1. A guest is defined as any non-club member brought onto club property by a member.

2. During non-hunting seasons, there are no guest restrictions.

3. All guests must be accompanied by a member while on club property. All guests 15 years of age and younger must be within view of the member while hunting any game.

Article VI
CARE OF PROPERTY

1. Each member will show the utmost courtesy and respect for the lease landowner and adjoining landowners' property. Gates must be kept closed at all times.

Article VII
FINANCES

1. The board of directors shall be authorized to make payment from club treasury all expenses necessary to operate the club. Any individual expense that exceeds $250.00 must be approved by 2/3 (67%) of club membership.

2. All checks written for Hunting Club must be signed by two (2) directors.

3. As of September 1 of each year, dues must be fully paid in order to maintain club membership.

Article VIII
AMENDMENTS

Any proposed change in bylaws must be approved by a majority vote of 3/4 (75%) of club members present at a called meeting.

Article IX
CLUB PRIDE

Hunting Club is more than a place to hunt – it is a fellowship of responsible sportsmen who belong to a special club. It is a privilege and an honor to be in the Club; each member should be cognizant and proud of this fact, and should do his fair share to make the club a better place for all.

Article X
RULES AND REGULATIONS

1. Rules and Regulations for Club and Amendments to these rules and regulations must be approved by 2/3 (67%) vote of the membership present at a called meeting.

2. Consumption of alcoholic beverages at any time of the day eliminates that member for the remainer of that day's hunt. Consumption of alcoholic beverages after 12:01 a.m. disqualifies any member from that day's hunt.

3. No firearm will be allowed in the camp house with a shell in the chamber or the magazine. No firearm will be allowed in the camp yard with a shell in the chamber. A muzzleloader must have the percussion cap removed from the nipple.

4. No trespassing on any adjacent landowner/club. If tracking a wounded deer, notify a board member (if present) or another member before crossing the property/club line.

5. All permanent deer stands will be marked on the stand map. Stands being hunted must be so indicated on the stand map.

6. Main roads (all vehicles, ATV roads, foot travel only roads, and parking areas will be designated on the club. No vehicle is to be used on any non-designated road except in an emergency or during workdays. ATV vehicles may be used on foot travel only roads to set up stands and/or retrieve deer.

7. A member should not knowingly go by a stand occupied by another member between daylight and 9:00 a.m. and between 3:30 p.m. and dark, except any stand located adjacent to an all-vehicle main road.

8. Tree stands will not be fastened to trees with any metal device, including, but not limited to, nails, screws, and wire, but may be tied to trees with rope. Chains and binders may be used to secure tree stands on a temporary basis, but these must be removed from the tree during the period of March 1st to September 1st of every year. This does include climbing stands!!

Appendix B   Sample Land Lease Agreement

This sample is for information only and not a substitute for legal counsel since statutes pertaining to leasing vary from state to state.

This lease is entered into by and between _____ , hereinafter referred to as "Lessor" and _____ , hereinafter referred to as "Lessee." By doing so, each agrees to the following provisions:

#1

Lessor does hereby lease, for the term and amount as per provisions #2 and #3, and subject to the reservations and conditions hereinafter set forth, the exclusive right to hunt on the following described tract of land located in _____ County, _____ State, and described as follows: *(Legal Description)*

_____

_____

_____

#2

This lease shall be for a term of _____ years, commencing _____(date)_____and terminating _____(date)_____ unless sooner terminated pursuant to provisions of this agreement hereinafter set forth. Either the Lessor or the Lessee may cancel this agreement by giving written notice of its intent to do so ninety (90) days prior to the date that payment for the next year is due. In which event, Lessee shall be relieved of the obligation to pay further lease payments under the terms hereof and shall deliver possession of the premises.

#3

The consideration for which this lease is granted is an annual cash payment to be paid as follows, to-wit:

$_____ on execution hereof;

$_____on_____(date)_____;

$_____on_____(date)_____;

#4

Lessee agrees that it will not transfer, assign, or sublease in whole or in part this lease.

#5

Lessee agrees that all property of every kind, that may be on the premises during the continuance of this lease, whether, same is property of Lessor or Lessee, shall be there at the sole risk of Lessee. Lessor shall not be liable to Lessee or to any other person for any injury, loss, or damage regardless of the nature thereof to any person or property on the leased premises. Lessee agrees to indemnify and hold harmless Lessor against any and all liability whatsoever for damages to any person or thing because of personal injury or property damage arising out of or resulting from Lessee's use and enjoyment of the privileges herein granted, whether said personal injury or property damage should result from accident, use of firearms, or otherwise occurring on the leased premises during or connected with any hunting, or any other activity organized or conducted by Lessee, its members, guests, servants or employees. In this connection, it is agreed that one of the terms and conditions under which the above premises is leased is that the Lessee assumes responsibility for the conditions of the premises and for any occurrences which happen thereon, including use of roads or other facilities constructed or maintained by Lessor.

Lessee shall, at Lessee's own expense, carry insurance for the duration of the lease as follows:

Comprehensive General Liability with minimum limits of $500,000 per person and $1,000,000 per occurrence for bodily injury and $150,000 for property damage.

A certificate indicating this insurance is in effect and a statement that the insurance carrier will not cancel without giving the Lessor 30 days notice must be filed with Lessor and shall be subject to Lessor's approval.

#6

Lessee will report all game harvested to the Lessor in order that long-term wildlife management programs may be carried out on the property.

#7

Lessee may camp or erect any type structure on this tract only after written approval of Lessor is obtained.

#8

Lessee agrees to take good care of the property and will be responsible for any damage to fields, farm equipment, livestock, fences, trees, roads, or structures.

#9

Lessee agrees to exercise extreme care in order that wild fires are avoided and to aid in the prevention and suppression of any fires encountered on the tract. All forest or grass fires will be reported to the county forest ranger promptly.

#10

The Lessee will abide by all county, state, and federal laws regarding hunting and fishing. Lessee shall be responsible for the conduct of Lessee's club members or guests. Any violation of the laws shall be considered just cause for immediate cancellation of this lease by Lessor, and no prorations of the lease payment previously paid shall be made.

#11

Lessee acknowledges that Lessor owns this tract of land primarily for the growing of agricultural crops and/or forest and Lessee shall not interfere with Lessor's forest management or farming operation. Lessor reserves the right in its sole discretion at any time to perform farming or forestry operations upon any or all portions of this tract. At any time there are forest management or farming workers on this tract, there will be a 300-yard "no hunting" zone in effect around the work area.

#12

Lessee agrees that it shall limit the total number of hunters on the tract at one time to one hunter per acre. All hunters must have on their person written permission to hunt signed by the Lessee.

#13

Lessee agrees that no nails, spikes, or metal objects will be screwed or driven into any trees on the premises for any purpose whatsoever, except that trees along property line may be used for boundary posting purposes, provided aluminum nails are used.

All hunting stands shall be portable and shall not be permanently affixed to or built in trees.

#14

Lessor reserves and shall have the right of ingress and egress into, over, and across the said lands during the term of this lease at any time and for any reason it may deem necessary or desirable. Lessor further reserves the right to build or to grant rights of way over, on, or under the leased premises for purpose which Lessor deems necessary.

#15

Lessee shall not construct any roads, food plots, or other improvements, or make alterations on said lands without prior written consent of Lessor.

#16

Lessor reserves the right to deny access to the leased premises to any person or persons for any of the following reasons: carelessness with guns, violations of game and fish laws, trespassing on property of adjoining landowners, acts which could reasonably be expected to strain relations with adjoining landowners, acts which hinder forestry or farming operations on Lessor or its grantees, or any other activities which to the ordinary person would be considered unsafe, objectionable, offensive, or to cause embarrassment to Lessor or be detrimental to the Lessor's interest. Failure of Lessee to expel or deny access to the premises to any person or persons after being notified to do so by Lessor may result in the termination of this lease at discretion of Lessor.

#17

Modifications of this lease shall be made in writing and signed copies of same will be attached to the original lease.

#18
Special Provisions:

_____

_____

_____

_____

_____

_____

Thus done and signed on this_____ day of _____, 20_____ in the presence of the undersigned witnesses.

Witnesses:

_____

_____

Witnesses:

_____

_____

Lessor:

_____

Lessor:

_____

Appendix C Sample Release of Liability and Acknowledgment of Dangers, Risks, and Hazards of Hunting or Visiting on Hunt Club

(Holly Creek Hunting Club, Boone County, NC)

This is my acknowledgment that this document is sufficient warning that natural and man-made dangerous conditions, risks, and hazards do exist on this property. My presence and activities on the premises expose me and my property to dangerous conditions, risks, and hazards, including but not limited to the following: elevated hunting stands, whether or not erected by the landowners; shooting activities; poisonous snakes, insects, and spiders; use of all-terrain vehicles and tractors; use of target throwing equipment; hazardous and dangerous driving and walking conditions; animals both wild and domesticated that may be potentially dangerous; deep and/or swift water; persons with firearms both on or off the premises; and the use of vehicles. I hereby state that I expressly assume all such dangers, risks, and hazards.

In consideration for the rights to enter the premises,

I hereby release and agree to protect, indemnify, and hold harmless the landowners and their respective agents, employees, employers, and assigns from and against any and all claims, demands, causes of action, and damages, including attorneys' fees, resulting from any accident, incident, or occurrence arising out of, incidental to, or in any way resulting from the use of the premises and improvements thereon, whether or not caused by the landowners' negligence or gross negligence. This release applies during the time that I am permitted on the premises. I hereby further covenant and agree that heirs, my successors, assigns, and I will not make any claim or institute any suit or action at law or in equity against the landowners or their respective heirs, agents, representatives, employees, successors, or assigns.

As used in this release, the terms **I**, **my person**, and **myself** include minors in my care while on the premises.

Thus done and signed on this_____ day of _____, 20_____ in the presence of the undersigned witnesses.

_____
(Signature)

_____
(Printed Name)

_____
(Address)

Appendix D Sample Cooperative Agreement

1. _____   _____
   (Landowner's Name)   *(Date)*

   _____   _____
   (Address)   *(Telephone Number)*

   _____
   (City)   *(State)*   *(Zip Code)*

2. I am the owner or authorized agent of tract or tracts of land located on county/state road

   _____ containing _____ acres,

   _____ containing _____ acres,

   _____ containing _____ acres,

3. I agree to cooperate with the goals and bylaws of the Cross Creek Deer Management Co-op.

4. This agreement does not give any unauthorized person the right to trespass on above listed property.

5. I am in no way obligated to the Cross Creek Deer Management Co-op. I agree with the management practices recommended and will require all hunting on my property to follow the agreed upon deer management plan.

6. This agreement is valid for the life of the co-op unless revoked in writing.

7. Annual membership dues are $5.00 which will be used for postage, advertisement, and educational programs.

_____

_____
(Signature of Landowner/Agent)

Appendix E Harvest Data Forms

Deer Harvest Record 20____

Property ID_____   Sheet ___ of ___

Deer #	Tag# (If Req.)	Date	Sex	Antler Data (Inches)						Weight (Pounds)		Age	Doe Lactating	Hunter Name
				Inside Spread	# of Points	R. Beam Length	L. Beam Length	R. Base Circ.	L. Base Circ.	Live	Field Dressed			

Appendix F-1 Game & Fish Agency Web Sites

Alabama
www.dcnr.state.al.us

Alaska
www.state.ak.us/local/akpages/FISH.GAME/ADFDHOME.HTMs

Arizona
www.gf.state.az.us

Arkansas
www.agfc.state.ar.us

California
www.dfg.ca.gov

Colorado
www.dnr.state.co.us

Connecticut
www.dep.state.ct.us/burnatr/wdhome.htm

Delaware
www.dnrec.state.de.us/fw/huntin1.htm

Florida
www.state.fl.us/gfc

Georgia
www.dnr.state.ga.us

Hawaii
www.hawaii.gov/dlnr

Idaho
www2.state.id.us/fishgame

Illinois
www.dnr.state.il.us

Indiana
www.state.in.us/dnr

Iowa
www.state.ia.us/government/dnr

Kansas
www.kdwp.state.ks.us

Kentucky
www.state.ky.us/agencies/fw/kdfwr.htm

Louisiana
www.wlf.state.la.us

Maine
www.state.me.us/ifw

Maryland
www.dnr.state.md.us

Massachusetts
www.state.ma.us/dfwele

Michigan
www.dnr.state.mi.us

Minnesota
www.dnr.state.mn.us

Mississippi
www.mdwfp.com

Missouri
www.conservation.state.mo.us

Montana
www.fwp.mt.gov

Nebraska
www.ngpc.state.ne.us

Nevada
www.state.nv.us/cnr/nvwildlife

New Hampshire
www.wildlife.state.nh.us

New Jersey
www.state.nj.us/dep/fgw

New Mexico
www.gmfsh.state.nm.us

New York
www.dec.state.ny.us/website/outdoors

North Carolina
www.state.nc.us/Wildlife

North Dakota
www.state.nd.us/gnf

Ohio
www.dnr.state.oh.us

Oklahoma
www.state.ok.us/™odwc

Oregon
www.dfw.state.or.us

Pennsylvania
www.dcnr.state.pa.us

Rhode Island
www.state.ri.us/dem

South Carolina
www.water.dnr.state.sc.us

South Dakota
www.state.sd.us/state/executive/gfp

Tennessee
www.state.tn.us/twra

Texas
www.tpwd.state.tx.us

Utah
www.nr.state.ut.us

Vermont
www.anr.state.vt.us

Virginia
www.dgif.state.va.us

Washington
www.wa.gov/wdfw

West Virginia
www.wvwildlife.com

Wisconsin
www.dnr.state.wi.us

Wyoming
www.gf.state.wy.us

Boone and Crockett Club
www.boone-crockett.org

Ducks Unlimited
www.ducks.org

National Rifle Association
www.nra.org

National Shooting Sports Foundation
www.nssf.org

National Wild Turkey Federation
www.nwtf.org

Pope and Young
www.pope-young.org

Quail Unlimited
www.qu.org

Quality Deer Management Association
www.qdma.org

Rocky Mountain Elk Foundation
www.rmef.org

Ruffed Grouse Society
rgshg@aol.com

United States Fish & Wildlife Service
www.fws.gov

Appendix F-2 Agencies Offering Free Game Management Assistance

Alabama
Wildlife Biologist
Natural Resources Conservation Service
Box 311
Auburn, AL 36830
Phone: 334-887-4535

Wildlife Department
Alabama Cooperative Extension Service
109 Duncan Hall
Auburn University, AL 36849
Phone: 334-844-4444

Wildlife Division
Alabama Division of Game and Fish
64 North Union St.
Montgomery, AL 36130
Phone: 334-242-3465

Alaska
Wildlife Biologist
Natural Resources Conservation Service
949 East 36th Ave., Suite 400
Anchorage, AK 99508-4362
Phone: 907-271-2424

Wildlife Department
Alaska State Extension Services
University of Alaska
Box 756180
Fairbanks, AK 99775-6180
Phone: 907-474-7246

Wildlife Division
Alaska Department of Game and Fish
Box 25526
Juneau, AK 99802-5526
Phone: 907-465-4100

Arizona
Wildlife Biologist
Natural Resources Conservation
3003 North Central Ave., Suite 800
Phoenix, AZ 85012-2945
Phone: 602-280-8808

Wildlife Department
Arizona State Extension Services
University of Arizona
Tucson, AZ 85721
Phone: 520-621-7209

Wildlife Division
Arizona Game and Fish Department
2221 West Greenway Rd.
Phoenix, AZ 85023
Phone: 602-942-3000

Arkansas
Wildlife Biologist
Natural Resources Conservation Service
Federal Office Building, Room 5404
700 West Capitol Ave.
Little Rock, AR 72201-3228
Phone: 501-324-5445

Wildlife Department
Arkansas State Extension Services
Box 391
Little Rock, AR 72203
Phone: 501-671-2001

Wildlife Division
Arkansas Game and Fish Commission
#2 Natural Resources Dr.
Little Rock, AR 72205
Phone: 501-223-6305

California
Wildlife Biologist
Natural Resources Conservation Service
2121-C Second St.
Davis, CA 95616-5475
Phone: 916-757-8215

Wildlife Department
California State Extension Services
Cooperative Extension and Agricultural
    Experiment Station
University of California
300 Lakeside Dr., Sixth Floor
Oakland, CA 94612-3560
Phone: 415-987-0060

Wildlife Division
California Department of Game and Fish
Box 944209
Sacramento, CA 94244-2090
Phone: 916-653-7664

Colorado
Wildlife Biologist
Natural Resources Conservation Service
655 Parfet St., Room E 200C
Lakewood, CO 80215-5517
Phone: 303-236-2886, ext. 202

Wildlife Department
Colorado State Extension Services
1 Administration Building
Colorado State University
Fort Collins, CO 80523
Phone: 970-491-6281

Wildlife Division
Colorado Division of Wildlife
6060 Broadway
Denver, CO 80216
Phone: 303-291-7208

Connecticut
Wildlife Biologist
Natural Resources Conservation Service
16 Professional Park Rd.
Storrs, CT 06268-1299
Phone: 203-487-4013

Wildlife Department
University of Connecticut
    Cooperative Extension
College of Agriculture
    and Natural Resources
Box U-87
Storrs, CT 06269-4087
Phone: 203-486-2840

Wildlife Division
Connecticut Department of
    Environmental Protection
State Office Building
79 Elm St.
Hartford, CT 06106-5127
Phone: 203-566-4522

Delaware
Wildlife Biologist
Natural Resources Conservation Service
1203 College Park Dr., Suite 101
Dover, DE 19904-8713
Phone: 302-678-4160

Wildlife Department
Delaware State Extension Service
University of Delaware
133 Townsend Hall
Newark, DE 19717-1303
Phone: 302-831-2504

Wildlife Division
Delaware Division of Fish and Wildlife
Box 1401
Dover, DE 19903
Phone: 302-739-5295

Florida
Wildlife Biologist
Natural Resources Conservation Service
2614 N.W. 43rd St.
Gainesville, FL 32606-6611
Phone: 903-338-9525

Wildlife Department
Florida State Extension Service
University of Florida
1038 McCarty Hall
Gainesville, FL 32611-0210
Phone: 904-392-1761

Wildlife Division
Florida Game and Fresh
    Water Fish Commission
Farris Bryant Building
620 South Meridian
Tallahassee, FL 32399-1600
Phone:904-488-2975

Georgia
Wildlife Biologist
Natural Resources Conservation Service
Federal Building, Box 13
355 East Hancock Avenue
Athens, GA 30601
Phone: 706-546-2272

Wildlife Department
Georgia State Extension Services
The University of Georgia
College of Agricultural
    and Environmental Sciences
Athens, GA 30602-7501
Phone: 706-542-3924

Wildlife Division
Georgia State Game and Fish Division
2070 U.S. Hwy 278 S.E.
Social Circle, GA 30279
Phone: 706-557-3020

Hawaii
Wildlife Biologist
Natural Resources Conservation Service
Box 50004
Honolulu, HI 96850-0002
Phone: 808-541-2601

Appendix F-2   Agencies Offering Free Game Management Assistance - continued

Wildlife Division
Hawaii Department of Land
    and Natural Resources
Box 621
Honolulu, HI 96809
Phone: 808-587-0400

Idaho
Wildlife Biologist
Natural Resources Conservation Service
3244 Elder St., Room 124
Boise, ID 83705
Phone: 208-378-5700

Wildlife Department
Idaho State Extension Services
University of Idaho
Cooperative Extension Service System
Moscow, ID 83843
Phone: 208-885-6356

Wildlife Division
Idaho Fish and Game Department
Box 25
Boise, ID 83707
Phone: 208-334-5159

Illinois
Wildlife Biologist
Natural Resources Conservation Service
1902 Fox Dr.
Champaign, IL 61820-7335
Phone: 217-398-5267

Wildlife Department
Illinois State Extension Services
University of Illinois
123 Mumford Hall
1301 West Gregory Dr.
Urbana, IL 61801
Phone: 217-333-5900

Wildlife Division
Illinois Department of Natural Resources
Lincoln Tower Plaza
524 South Second St.
Springfield, IL 62701-1787
Phone: 217-785-0075

Indiana
Wildlife Biologist
Natural Resources Conservation Service
6013 Lakeside Blvd.
Indianapolis, IN 46278-2933
Phone: 317-290-3200

Wildlife Department
Indiana State Extension Services
Purdue University
1140 Agriculture Administration Bldg.
West Lafayette, IN 47907-1104
Phone: 765-494-8489

Wildlife Division
Indiana Division of Game and Fish
402 West Washington St., Room W-273
Indianapolis, IN 46204-2212
Phone: 317-232-4080

Iowa
Wildlife Biologist
Natural Resources Conservation Service
693 Federal Building
210 Walnut St.
Des Moines, IA 50309-2180
Phone: 515-284-6655

Wildlife Department
Iowa State Extension Services
Iowa State University
315 Beardshear Hall
Ames, IA 50011
Phone: 515-294-6192

Wildlife Division
Iowa Department of Natural Resources
Wallace State Office Building
East Ninth and Grand Ave.
Des Moines, IA 50319-0034
Phone: 515-281-5145

Kansas
Wildlife Biologist
Natural Resources Conservation Service
760 South Broadway
Salina, KS 67401
Phone: 913-823-4565

Wildlife Department
Kansas State Extension Services
Kansas State University
127 Call Hall
Manhattan, KS 66506
Phone: 913-532-5734

Wildlife Division
Kansas Department of Wildlife and Parks
900 Jackson St., Ste. 502
Topeka, KS 66612-1220
Phone: 913-296-2281

Kentucky
Wildlife Biologist
Natural Resources Conservation Service
771 Corporate Dr. Suite 110
Lexington, KY 40503-5479
Phone: 606-224-7350

Wildlife Department
Kentucky State Extension Services
University of Kentucky
Lexington, KY 40546
Phone: 606-257-4302

Wildlife Division
Kentucky Department of Fish
    and Wildlife Resources
#1 Game Farm Rd.
Frankfort, KY 40601
Phone: 502-564-3400

Louisiana
Wildlife Biologist
Natural Resources Conservation Service
3737 Government St.
Alexandria, LA 71302-3727
Phone: 318-473-7751

Wildlife Department
Louisiana State Extension Services
Box 25100
Baton Rouge, LA 70894-5100
Phone: 504-388-6083

Wildlife Division
Louisiana Department
    of Wildlife and Fisheries
Box 98000
Baton Rouge, LA 70898
Phone: 504-765-2623

Maine
Wildlife Biologist
Natural Resources Conservation Service
5 Godfrey Dr.
Orono, ME, 04473
Phone: 207-866-7241

Wildlife Department
University of Maine
    Cooperative Extension
University of Maine
234 Nutting Hall
Orono, ME 04469
Phone: 207-581-2902

Wildlife Division
Maine Department of Inland
    Fisheries and Wildlife
284 State St., Station #41
Augusta, ME 04333
Phone: 207-287-5202

Maryland
Wildlife Biologist
Natural Resources Conservation Service
John Hanson Business Center
339 Busch's Frontage Rd., Suite 301
Annapolis, MD 21401-5534
Phone: 410-757-0861, ext. 315

Wildlife Department
Maryland State Extension Services
University of Maryland
1104 Symons Hall
College Park, MD 20742
Phone: 301-405-2072

Wildlife Division
Maryland Department
    of Natural Resources
Tawes State Office Building
Annapolis, MD 21401
Phone: 410-260-8540

Massachusetts
Wildlife Biologist
Natural Resources Conservation Service
451 West St.
Amherst, MA 01002-2995
Phone: 413-253-4351

Wildlife Department
Massachusetts State Extension Services
University of Massachusetts
Holdsworth Natural Resources Center
Amherst, MA 01003
Phone: 413-545-2665

Wildlife Division
Massachusetts Department of
    Fisheries, Wildlife, and Environmental
    Law Enforcement
100 Cambridge St.
Boston, MA 02202
Phone: 617-727-3155

Michigan
Wildlife Biologist
Natural Resources Conservation Service
1405 South Harrison Rd., Room 101
East Lansing, MI 48823-5243
Phone: 517-337-6701, ext. 1201

Appendix F-2   Agencies Offering Free Game Management Assistance - continued

Wildlife Department
Michigan State University Extension
10B Agriculture Hall
East Lansing, MI 48824-1039
Phone: 517-355-0240

Wildlife Division
Michigan Department
    of Natural Resources
Stevens T. Mason Building
Box 30028
Lansing, MI 48909
Phone: 517-373-2329

Minnesota
Wildlife Biologist
Natural Resources Conservation Service
600 Farm Credit Services Building
375 Jackson St.
St. Paul MN 555101-1854
Phone: 612-290-3675

Wildlife Department
Minnesota State Extension Services
University of Minnesota
240 Coffey Hall
1420 Eckles Ave.
St. Paul, MN 55108
Phone: 612-625-3774

Wildlife Division
Minnesota Department
    of Natural Resources
500 Lafayette Rd.
St. Paul, MN 55155-4020
Phone: 612-296-2549

Mississippi
Wildlife Biologist
Natural Resources Conservation Service
Federal Building, Suite 1321
100 Capitol Street
Jackson, MS 39269-1399
Phone: 601-965-5205

Wildlife Department
Mississippi State Extension Services
Mississippi State University
Mississippi State, MS 39762
Phone: 601-325-3036

Wildlife Division
Mississippi Department of Wildlife,
    Fisheries, and Parks
Box 451
Jackson, MS 39205
Phone: 601-364-2000

Missouri
Wildlife Biologist
Natural Resources Conservation Service
Parkade Center, Suite 250
601 Business Loop 70 West
Columbia, MO 65203-2546
Phone: 314-876-0900

Wildlife Department
Missouri State Extension Services
University of Missouri
309 University Hall
Columbia, MO 65211
Phone: 573-883-7754

Wildlife Division
Missouri Department of Conservation
Box 180
Jefferson City, MO 65102-0180
Phone: 573-751-4115

Montana
Wildlife Biologist
Natural Resources Conservation Service
Federal Building
10 East Babcock St., Room 443
Bozeman, MT 59715-4704
Phone: 406-587-6813

Wildlife Department
Montana State Extension Services
Montana State University
Linfield Hall
Bozeman, MT 59717
Phone: 406-994-6647

Wildlife Division
Montana Department of
    Fish, Wildlife, and Parks
1420 East Sixth Ave.
Helena, MT 59620
Phone: 406-444-3186

Nebraska
Wildlife Biologist
Natural Resources Conservation Service
Federal Building, Room 152
100 Centennial Mall North
Lincoln, NE 68508-3866
Phone: 402-437-5300

Wildlife Department
Nebraska State Extension Services
University of Nebraska
Lincoln, NE 68583-0703
Phone: 402-472-2966

Wildlife Division
Nebraska Game and Parks Commission
Box 30370
Lincoln, NE 68503
Phone: 402-471-5539

Nevada
Wildlife Biologist
Natural Resources Conservation Service
5301 Langley Lane, Building F
Suite 201
Reno, NV 89511
Phone: 702-784-5863

Wildlife Department
Nevada State Extension Services
University of Nevada
1000 Valley Rd.
Reno, NV 89512
Phone: 702-784-4020

Wildlife Division
Nevada Department of Conservation
    and Natural Resources
1100 Valley Rd.
Reno, NV 89512
Phone: 702-688-1599

New Hampshire
Wildlife Biologist
Natural Resources Conservation Service
Federal Building
2 Madbury Rd.
Durham, NH 03824
Phone: 603-433-0505

Wildlife Department
University of New Hampshire
    Cooperative Extension
Taylor Hall
59 College Road
Durham, NH 03824-2618
Phone: 603-862-3594

Wildlife Division
New Hampshire Fish and Game Department
2 Hazen Dr.
Concord, NH 03301
Phone: 603-271-3422

New Jersey
Wildlife Biologist
Natural Resources Conservation Service
1370 Hamilton St.
Somerset, NJ 08873-3157
Phone: 908-246-1205

Wildlife Department
New Jersey State Extension Services
Rutgers State University Cook College
Box 231
New Brunswick, NJ 08903
Phone: 732-932-9306

Wildlife Division
New Jersey Division of Fish,
    Game and Wildlife
CN 400
Trenton, NJ 08625
Phone: 609-292-9410

New Mexico
Wildlife Biologist
Natural Resources Conservation Service
6200 Jefferson St. N.E.
Albuquerque, MN 87109
Phone: 505-761-4400

Wildlife Department
New Mexico State Extension Services
New Mexico State University
Box 30003 Campus Box 3AG
Las Cruces, NM 88003
Phone: 505-646-3748

Wildlife Division
New Mexico Natural Resource Department
Villagra Building
Santa Fe, NM 87503
Phone: 505-827-7911

New York
Wildlife Biologist
Natural Resources Conservation Service
441 South Salina St.
Suite 354
Syracuse, NY 13202-2450
Phone: 315-477-6504

Appendix F-2   Agencies Offering Free Game Management Assistance - continued

Wildlife Department
New York State Cooperative Extension
Cornell University
NY State College of Agriculture and
   Life Sciences and Human Ecology
276 Roberts Hall
Ithaca, NY 14853-4203
Phone: 607-255-2237

Wildlife Division
New York Department of
   Environmental Conservation
50 Wolf Rd.
Albany, NY 12233
Phone: 518-474-2121

North Carolina
Wildlife Biologist
Natural Resources Conservation Service
4405 Bland Rd., Suite 205
Raleigh, NC 27609-6293
Phone: 919-873-2102

Wildlife Department
North Carolina Cooperative
   Extension Services
North Carolina State University
Box 7602
Raleigh, NC 27695
Phone: 919-55-2811

Wildlife Division
North Carolina Wildlife
   Resources Commission
Archdale Building
512 North Salisbury St.
Raleigh, NC 27601-1188
Phone: 919-733-3391

North Dakota
Wildlife Biologist
Natural Resources Conservation Service
Box 1458
Bismarck, ND 58502-1458
Phone: 701-250-4421

Wildlife Department
North Dakota State Extension Service
North Dakota State University
Box 5437
Fargo, ND 58105
Phone: 701-231-7173

Wildlife Division
North Dakota State Game
   and Fish Department
100 North Bismarck Expressway,
Bismarck, ND 58501
Phone: 701-221-6300

Ohio
Wildlife Biologist
Natural Resources Conservation Service
200 North High St., Room 522
Columbus, OH 43215-2748
Phone: 614-469-6962

Wildlife Department
Ohio State University Extension Services
2120 Fyffe Rd.
Columbus, OH 43210
Phone: 614-292-4067

Wildlife Division
Ohio Division of Wildlife
1840 Belcher Dr.
Columbus, OH 43224-1329
Phone: 614-265-6300

Oklahoma
Wildlife Biologist
Natural Resources Conservation Service
100 USDA Agriculture Center Building
Suite 203
Stillwater, OK 64074-2624
Phone: 405-742-1200

Wildlife Department
Oklahoma State Extension Services
Oklahoma State University
Agricultural Hall, Room 139
Stillwater, OK 74078
Phone: 405-744-5398

Wildlife Division
Oklahoma Department
   of Wildlife Conservation
Box 53465
Oklahoma City, OK 73152
Phone: 405-521-3851

Oregon
Wildlife Biologist
Natural Resources Conservation Service
101 S.W. Main St., Suite 1300
Portland, OR 97104-3221
Phone: 503-414-3201

Wildlife Department
Oregon State Extension Services
Oregon State University
Corvallis, OR 97331
Phone: 541-737-2713

Wildlife Division
Oregon Department of Fish and Wildlife
Box 59
Portland, OR 97207
Phone: 503-229-5410 ext. 401

Pennsylvania
Wildlife Biologist
Natural Resources Conservation Service
One Credit Union Pl., Suite 340
Wildwood Center
Harrisburg, PA 17110-2993
Phone: 717-782-2202

Wildlife Department
Pennsylvania State Extension Services
Pennsylvania State University
201 Agricultural Administration Bldg.
University Park, PA 16802-2600
Phone: 814-865-2541

Wildlife Division
Pennsylvania Game Commission
2001 Elmerton Ave.
Harrisburg, PA 17110-9797
Phone: 717-787-3633

Rhode Island
Wildlife Biologist
Natural Resources Conservation Service
60 Quaker Lane, Suite 46
Warwick, RI 02886-0111
Phone: 401-828-1300

Wildlife Department
Rhode Island State
   Cooperative Extension Services
University of Rhode Island
Kingston, RI 02881
Phone: 401-874-2599

Wildlife Division
Rhode Island Department of
   Environmental Management
Stedman Government Center
4808 Tower Hill Rd.
Wakefield, RI 02879
Phone: 401-277-3075

South Carolina
Wildlife Biologist
Natural Resources Conservation Service
Strom Thurmond Federal Building
1835 Assembly St., Rm. 950
Columbia, SC 29201-2489
Phone: 803-765-5681

Wildlife Department
South Carolina State Extension Services
Clemson University
Clemson, SC 29634-0310
Phone: 864-656-3382

Wildlife Division
South Carolina Department
   of Natural Resources
Rembert C. Dennis Building
Box 167
Columbia, SC 29202
Phone: 803-734-4007

South Dakota
Wildlife Biologist
Natural Resources Conservation Service
Federal Building
200 4th St. S.W.
Huron, SD 57350
Phone: 605-352-1200

Wildlife Department
South Dakota State Extension Services
South Dakota State University
Box 2207D
Brookings, SD 57007
Phone: 605-688-4792

Wildlife Division
South Dakota Department of Game,
   Fish, and Parks
Siqurd Anderson Building
523 East Capitol
Pierre, SD 57501-3182
Phone: 605-773-3387

Tennessee
Wildlife Biologist
Natural Resources Conservation Service
675 U.S. Courthouse
801 Broadway St.
Nashville, TN 37203-3878
Phone: 615-736-5471

Appendix F-2   Agencies Offering Free Game Management Assistance - continued

Wildlife Department
Tennessee State Extension Services
University of Tennessee
Agricultural Extension Service
Box 1071
Knoxville, TN 37901-1071
Phone: 423-974-7114

Wildlife Division
Tennessee Wildlife Resources Agency
Ellington Agricultural Center
Box 40747
Nashville, TN 37204
Phone: 615-781-6552

Texas
Wildlife Biologist
Natural Resources Conservation Service
W. R. Poage Federal Building
101 South Main Street
Temple, TX 76501-7682
Phone: 817-774-1214

Wildlife Department
Texas Agricultural Extension Service
Texas A&M University
College Station, TX 77843-7101
Phone: 409-845-7967

Wildlife Division
Texas Parks and Wildlife Department
4200 Smith School Rd.
Austin, TX 78744
Phone: 512-389-4802

Utah
Wildlife Biologist
Natural Resources Conservation Service
125 South State St., Room 4002
Salt Lake City, UT 84138-0350
Phone: 801-524-5050

Wildlife Department
Utah State Extension Services
Utah State University
Logan, UT 84322-4900
Phone: 801-797-2201

Wildlife Division
Utah State Division of Wildlife Resources
1596 WN Temple
Salt Lake City, UT 84116-3154
Phone: 801-538-4702

Vermont
Wildlife Biologist
Natural Resources Conservation Service
69 Union Street
Winooski, VT 05404-1999
Phone: 802-951-6796

Wildlife Department
University of Vermont Extension
601 Main St.
Burlington, VT 05401-3439
Phone: 802-656-2990

Wildlife Division
Vermont Fish and Game Department
103 South Main St., 10 South
Waterbury, VT 05671-0501
Phone: 805-241-3730

Virginia
Wildlife Biologist
Natural Resources Conservation Service
Culpepper Building
1606 Santa Rose Rd., Suite 209
Richmond, VA 23229-5014
Phone: 804-287-1691

Wildlife Department
Virginia State Extension Services
Virginia Polytechnic and State University
Blacksburg, VA 24061-0402
Phone: 540-231-5299

Wildlife Division
Virginia Department
  of Game and Inland Fisheries
4010 West Broad St.
Richmond, VA 23230-1104
Phone: 804-367-9231

Washington
Wildlife Biologist
Natural Resources Conservation Service
Rock Point Tower 2, Suite 450
West 316 Boone Ave.
Spokane, WA 99201-2348
Phone: 509-353-2337

Wildlife Department
Washington State Extension Services
Washington State University
Box 646230
Pullman, WA 99164-6230
Phone: 509-335-2933

Wildlife Division
Washington Department
  of Fish and Wildlife
600 Capitol Way North
Olympia, WA 98501-1091
Phone: 360-753-5710

West Virginia
Wildlife Biologist
Natural Resources Conservation Service
75 High St., Room 301
Morgantown, WV 26505
Phone: 304-291-4153

Wildlife Department
West Virginia State Extension Services
West Virginia University
817 Knapp Hall
Morgantown, WV 26506
Phone: 304-293-5691

Wildlife Division
West Virginia Division
  of Natural Resources
1900 Kanawha Blvd. East
Charleston, WV 25305
Phone: 304-558-2771

Wisconsin
Wildlife Biologist
Natural Resources Conservation Service
6515 Watts Rd., Suite 200
Madison, WI 53719-2726
Phone: 608-264-5341, ext. 122

Wildlife Department
University of Wisconsin Extension
432 North Lake St.
Madison WI 53706
Phone: 608-263-2775

Wildlife Division
Wisconsin Department
  of Natural Resources
Box 7921
Madison, WI 53707
Phone: 608-266-2121

Wyoming
Wildlife Biologist
Natural Resources Conservation Service
Federal Office Bldg.
100 East B. St. Room 3124
Casper, WY 82601
Phone: 307-261-6453

Wildlife Department
Wyoming State Extension Services
University Station
Box 3354
Laramie, WY 82071
Phone: 307-766-5124

Wildlife Division
Wyoming Game and Fish Department
5400 Bishop Blvd.
Cheyenne, WY 82006
Phone: 307-777-4601

Appendix F-3 Mapping Programs

myTOPO.com
P.O. Box 2075, Red lodge, MT 59068
Phone: 877-587-9004
www.mytopo.com

DeLorme
Phone: 800-569-8313
www.delorme.com

U.S. Gelogical Survey
P.O. Box 25286, Denver, CO 80225
Phone: 888-ask-usgs
www.usgs.gov

Appendix F-4 Wildlife Seed Sources

Adams Briscoe Seed Co.
Box 19, Jackson, GA 30233
Phone: 770-775-7826

C.P. Daniel's Sons, Inc.
Box 119, Waynesboro, GA 30830
Phone: 1-800-822-5681

Haile-Dean Seed Co.
501 North Hennis Rd.
Winter Garden, FL 34787
Phone: 1-800-423-7333

E.A. Hauss Nursery
4165 Ross Rd., Atmore, AL 36502
Phone: 334-368-4854

National Wild Turkey Federation
Box 530, Edgefield, SC 29824
Phone: 1-800-843-6983

Osenbaugh Grass Seeds
RR 1, Box 44, Lucas, IA 50151
Phone: 515-766-6792

Pennington Seed Co.
Box 290, Madison, GA 30650
Phone: 1-800-277-1412

Sharp Brothers Seed Co.
396 S.W. Davis St.-Ladue
Clinton, MO 65735
660-885-7551

Spandle Nurseries
Tr. 2, Box 125, Claxton, GA 30417
Phone: 1-800-553-5771

Whitetail Institute
Rt. 1, Box 3006, Pintlala, AL 36043

Texas Seed Co.
Drawer 599, Kennedy, TX 78119
Phone: 1-800-321-5673

The Wildlife Group
2858 County Rd. 53, Tuskegee, AL 36083
Phone: 1-800-221-9703

Appendix F-5 Insurance Sources

Davis-Garvin Agency, Inc.

Quality Deer Management Association

Forest Landowners Association, Inc.

National Rifle Association Hunt Club Insurance

Outdoorsman Agency

Buckmasters Liability Insurance

Maryland Forest Association

Outdoor Underwriters, Inc.

Appendix F-6 Wildlife Management Tools Sources

Ben Meadows
P.O. Box 5277
Jamesville, WI 53547-5277

Wildlife Enterprises
22 Laurel Way
Kerryville, TX 78028
Phone: 830-257-4538

Forestry Suppliers, Inc.
Box 8397, Jackson, MS 39284
Phone: 800-647-5368

Interstate Graphics, Inc.
7817 Burden Rd., Rockford, IL 61115
Phone: 1-800-243-3925

Minuteman Signs
Box 457, Pfafftown, NC 27040

Signs by John Voss
Box 553, Manlius, NY 13104
Phone: 315-682-6418

Quality Deer Management Association (QDMA)
7500-C Macon Highway
Watkinsville, GA 30677
Phone: 1-800-209-3337

Appendix F-7 Shooting Range Development Assistance

National Shooting Sports Foundation
Range Development
11 Mile Hill Road
Newtown, CT 06470-2359
Phone: 203-426-1320
Website: www.rangeinfo.org

National Rifle Association
Range Development
11250 Waples Mill Rd.
Fairfax, VA 22030-7400
Phone: 703-267-1595
Website: www.nra.org

Appendix F-8 Sources of Hunting Club Cabins *(Lob Cabin Kits)*

Appalachian Log Homes, Inc
11312 Station West Drive
Knoxville, TN 37922
Phone: 1-800-726-0708
www.alhloghomes.com

Heritage Log Homes, Inc.
P. O. Box 8080
Sevierville, TN 37864
Phone: 1-800-456-4663
www.heritagelog.com

Honest Abe Log Homes, Inc.
3855 Clay County Highway
Moss, TN 38575
Phone: 1-800-231-3695
www.honestabe.com

Kuhns Brothers Log Homes
390 Swartz Road
Lewisburg, PA 17837
Phone: 800-326-9614
www.kuhnsbros.com

Northeastern Log Homes
P.O. Box 126
Groton, VT 05046-0126
Phone: 1-800-992-6526
www.northeasternlog.com

Northeastern Log Homes
P. O. Box 46
Kenduskeag, ME 04450-0046
Phone: 1-800-624-2797

Northeastern Log Homes
1126 Southampton Rd.
Westfield, MA 01085-1368
Phone: 1-800-528-4456

Northeastern Log Homes
P.O. Box 7966
Louisville, KY 40257-0966
Phone: 1-800-451-2724

Panel Concepts, Inc.
331 No. M-33
Mio, MI 48647
Phone: 989-826-6511
www.panelconcepts.com

Suwannee River Log Homes
4345 U.S. 90
Wellborn, FL 32094
www.srloghomes.com

Tennessee Log Homes
2537 Decatur Pike
Athens, TN 37303
Phone: 800-251-9218 • 423-744-8156
www.tnloghomes.com

Ward Log Homes
P.O. Box 72
Houlton, ME 04730
Phone: 800-341-1566
www.wardloghomes.com

The Wilderness Cabin Co.
415 Neave Court
Kelowna, BC Canada V1V 2M2
Phone: 1-888-891-3111/250-765-0535
www.wildernesscabin.com

Appendix F-9 Standard Shutdown Camp Rules *(Fox Ridge Hunting & Shooting Club)*

1. Make sure all shooting ranges are clean and range/sporting clays houses are left clean and neat.

   All brass, including .22 rimfire cases and shot shell hulls should be removed. Used targets should be taken down and carried out with garbage.

2. Replace anything you use: firewood, kindling, propane, kerosene, Coleman fuel, gasoline, food, drinks, water, etc. Leave the wood box and kindling baskets full.

3. Remove ashes from stove and clean up the mess made emptying ashes. Leave stove ready to light.

4. Refill the lanterns with appropriate fuel.

5. Collect garbage from cabin, woodshed, and shooting range and replace garbage bags. Take the garbage out with you.

6. Wipe the table and countertops clean.

7. Sweep cabin floor, porch, outhouse, and bench area of range house thoroughly.

8. Bring the porch chairs inside.

9. Leave the dishes clean and put away.

10. Hang the wet dishtowels so they can dry.

11. Close and lock the cabin windows and pull shades.

12. Make sure the range equipment is put away and covers are on the sporting clays machines.

13. Range house doors should be closed with snaps in place.

14. All perishable foods should be taken out, and any nonperishable foods that are left over should be sealed tightly.

15. Make sure all doors and gates are left locked.

16. *If you eat it, drink it, burn it, break it, or use it, replace it. If you get it dirty, clean it.*

Appendix F-10 Standard Operating Procedures (Fox Ridge Hunting & Shooting Club)

1. Keep vehicle use to a minimum to prevent damage to roads and fields.

2. Vehicles should not be taken inside cabin fence unless absolutely necessary.

3. Remember that clay target throwers can be extremely dangerous. Only responsible adults should use target throwers or be inside target thrower houses: absolutely no children are allowed inside houses for any reason. Bring your own clay targets.

4. Ear and eye protection are required of both shooters and spectators for all shooting activities.

5. No target practice is to be done on the property except on designated ranges.

6. Shotgun pattern boards are for shotguns firing lead shot only. No rifles, pistols, or steel shot may be used.

7. On rifle, pistol, and pattern board ranges, only one shooter at a time should be on the firing line. All other firearms should be left in the rack unloaded.

8. No breakable objects such as soft drink bottles are to be used as targets.

9. On sporting clays course, only one position is to be used at a time, and only one shooter at a time should be in shooting position. All other shooters should have shotguns unloaded and actions open.

10. All state and federal game laws must be obeyed. All special hunting regulations imposed by owners must be obeyed.

11. Absolutely no hunting or fishing by anyone without permission.

12. Keep all gates closed and locked at all times, unless the owner states differently.

13. No smoking inside cabin. If you must smoke outside, do not throw cigarette butts on ground.

14. Never leave the front of the stove open without the fire screen in place. Do not leave the cabin with front of stove open, even with fire screen.

15. Never use any flammable fuel as a fire starter.

16. Never fill the stove with lighter wood; use only a few pieces to start a fire, and then add split firewood. Filling the stove with lighter wood will cause intense heat and result in a cabin fire.

17. Never burn trash in the stove.

18. If using the generator, be sure to check the oil level with each use.

19. After using the cook stove, make sure the burners are turned **off**.

20. Do not set hot pots and pans on countertops or table without pads.

21. Do not put anything but human waste and toilet paper in the outhouse pit. Toilet paper rolls, sanitary napkins, cigarette butts, and garbage of any kind go into the cabin trash.

22. Use lime in the outhouse–every time.

23. Upon leaving the outhouse, leave the toilet seat down.

24. Chairs are not to be left on the porch.

25. Do not cut trees, bushes, flowers, etc., without permission.

26. Any problems or suspected problems should be reported to the owners promptly.

27. No guests except those invited by owners.

28. To be a guest and use the club facilities, you must sign a liability release form.

29. Bring your own sleeping bag or sheets and blankets, towels, etc.

30. Deer harvest: Only one buck per guest per year, and it must be eight points or better with a spread outside the ears. If you will not have it mounted, do not shoot it.

31. To hunt doe deer, you must have a DMP tag.

32. Data must be taken from bucks and does per the DMP Program.

Appendix F-11 ATV Food Plot Accessories

Woods-N-Water
311 North Marcus St.
Wrightsville, GA 31096
Phone: 888-440-9108
www.theplotmaster.com

BushMaster Jr.
800 South Industrial Pkwy.
Yazoo, MS 39194
Phone: 877-647-2563
www.amcomfg.com

EarthWay Seeders
1009 Maple St.
Bristol, IN 46506
Phone: 574-848-7491
www.earthway.com

Cycle Country
2188 Hwy 86
Milford, IA 51351
Phone; 800-841-2222
www.cyclecountry.com

Panorama Harrow
P.O. Box 415
523 South Sangamon Ave.
Gibson Ciy, IL 80936
Phone: 800-392-2386

Monroe-Tufline Mfg. Co.
P. O. Box 186
Columbus, MS 39703
Phone: 662-328-8347
www.monroetufline.com

Fuerst
1020 South Sangamon Ave.
Gibson City, IL 60936
Phone : 800-435-9630
www.fuerst-bros.com

Index